NEW POETRY
OF MEXICO

NEW POETRY OF MEXICO

Selected, with notes, by
OCTAVIO PAZ
ALI CHUMACERO,
JOSE EMILIO PACHECO,
and HOMERO ARIDJIS

Bilingual edition edited by
MARK STRAND

Secker & Warburg · London

First published in England 1972 by
Martin Secker & Warburg Limited
14 Carlisle Street, London W1V 6NN

Printed offset litho in Great Britain by
Cox & Wyman Ltd
London, Fakenham and Reading

Grateful acknowledgment is made to the following for permission
to reprint copyright material:
Paul Blackburn, for his translation of Octavio Paz, 'Viento Intero',
which first appeared in *Latin American Writing Today*, edited by
J. M. Cohen and published by Penguin Books Ltd.
Rachel Benson, for her translations of Xavier Villaurrutia, 'Nocturno
eterno' and José Gorostiza, 'Muerte sin fin' which first appeared in
Las Americas.

Assistance for the translation was given by the
Center for Inter-American Relations.

SBN: 436 36480 8 (cloth)
     436 36481 6 (paper)

CONTENTS

6

8

FROM OCTAVIO PAZ'S INTRODUCTION TO THE MEXICAN EDITION

The expression "Mexican poetry" is ambiguous: is it poetry written by Mexicans or poetry that in some manner reveals the spirit, the reality, or the character of Mexico? Our poets write twentieth-century Mexican Spanish but the *Mexicanness* of their poems as reflecting national character is very doubtful. It is said that López Velarde is the most Mexican of our poets, yet his work is so personal in style that it would be useless to look for someone like him among his contemporaries and descendants. If that is what determines one's *Mexicanness*, then we would have to conclude that *Mexicanness* consists in not appearing like any other Mexican. It would not be a general characteristic without personal anomaly.

The fact is that the work of López Velarde bears more than a slight resemblance to the work of the Argentine poet Lugones, which, in its time, seemed close to the work of Laforgue. Not national character but the spirit of an epoch unites these three poets. This observation is applicable to other literatures: Manrique seems more like Villon than Garcilaso, and Góngora is closer to Marino than to Berceo. The existence of a French or a German or an English poetry is debatable; but the reality of Baroque, Romantic, or Symbolist poetry is not. While I do not deny national traditions or the temperament of peoples, I believe that styles are universal or, rather, international. What we call national traditions are, almost always, versions and adaptations of universal styles. Finally, a work is something more than a tradition and a style: it is a unique creation, a singular vision. The more perfect a work is, the less visible its tradition and style. Art aspires to clarity.

The poetry of Mexicans is part of a larger tradition: that of the poetry of the Spanish language written in Spanish America in the modern epoch. This tradition is not the same as that of Spain. Our tradition is also and above all a polemical style, at war constantly with the Spanish tradition and with itself: Spanish purism against cosmopolitanism; its own cosmopolitanism against a will to be American. As soon as this desire for style asserted itself, to part with "modernism," it set up a dialogue between Spain and Spanish America. That dialogue is the history of our poetry: Darío and Jiménez, Machado and Lugones, Huidobro and Guillén, Neruda and García Lorca. Mexican poets have participated in this dialogue since the time of Gutiérrez Najera and the *Revista Azul*. Without that dialogue there would be no modern poets in Mexico, but also, without the Mexicans the poetry of our language would not be what it is.

I underline the Spanish American character of our authors because I believe that the poetry written in our country is part of a general movement begun around 1885 in the Spanish portion of America. There is no Argentine, Mexican, or Venezuelan poetry: there is a Spanish American poetry or, more exactly, a Spanish American tradition and style. The national histories of our literature are as artificial as our political frontiers. Both are a consequence of the great failure of the wars of independence. Our liberators and their successors divided us. But what our leaders separated may through poetry be united. Our book thus presents only a fragment, the Mexican part, of South American poetry. This national limitation, however antipathetic it seems, is not too serious. Our book is nothing if not a contribution to the Spanish American dialogue.

If the criterion of nationality seems insufficient to me, what can be said of the prejudice for modernism? I say prejudice because that is the way things are. Prejudice is inseparable from our being: modernism for the last hundred years has been our style. It is the universal style. To want to be modern seems crazy: we are condemned to be modern, since the future and the past are prohibited us. But modernism does not consist in resigning oneself to live through this weird period we call the twentieth century. Modernism is a decision—a desire not to be like those who preceded us and a wish to be the beginning of another time. Ancient wisdom preached to live the moment—a unique moment but, nevertheless, identical to all those moments that preceded it. Modernism states that the moment is unique because it does not appear like the others: there is nothing new under the sun, except the creations and inventions of man; nothing is new on the earth, ex-

cept that each day man changes. That which distinguishes
the moment from all other moments is its cargo of an un-
known future. Not repetition but inauguration; severance and
not continuity. The modern tradition is the tradition of sever-
ance. Illusory or not, this idea fired up the young Rubén
Darío and he used it to proclaim a new aesthetic. The second
great movement of the century began also as severance: Hui-
dobro and the Ultraists violently denied the immediate past.

The process is circular: the search for the future always
ends with the reconquest of the past. That past is no less new
than the future: it is a past reinvented. Each instant gives
birth to a past and extinguishes a future. This tradition is also
an invention of "the modern." Or said differently: modernism
shapes its past with the same violence that it builds its future
—castles in the air, no less fantastic and vulnerable than the
timeless buildings of other epochs. In short, our prejudice is
more a position than an aesthetic, more a consciousness than
a destiny. We mean to use the time that is given to us not as
something imposed but as something wanted—a time that
seems like no other time and which is always, with its ca-
cophonies and repetitions, the incarnation of the unforeseen.
Modernism is born of desperation and is perpetually en-
amored of the unexpected. Its glory and its grief are not of this
world; they are the marvels and the reproaches of the future.
Our book attempts to reflect the trajectory of modernism in
Mexico: poetry on the move, poetry in revolt.

Anthologies aim to present the best poems of an author or
of the period and, in this way, they imply a more or less
static view of literature. But if I admit that tastes change,
criticism asserts that almost always works remain; though the
vision of one critic be different from that of other critics, the
territory they consider is the same. This book is inspired by a
distinct idea: the territory also changes. Works are never the
same, readers are authors as well. The works that inspire us
with passion are those that transform themselves indefinitely;
the poems that we love are mechanisms of successive
meaning—an architecture that unmakes and remakes itself
without stopping, an organism in perpetual revolution. Not
quiet beauty, but mutations and transmutations. A poem does
not mean, but engenders meaning: it is language in its purest
form.

Uncertainty of the considered landscape and uncertainty of point of view: to read Segovia or Sabines from the point of view of a reader of González Martínez is not the same as to read Tablada or Gorostiza from the viewpoint of a reader of Montes de Oca or Aridjis. In the first case our point of view would be static: we see the present from a completed past. In the second, we see the past from a present in motion: the past imperceptibly survives changes, marches toward us.

In general, criticism looks for the continuity of a literature apart from its established authors. It sees the past as a beginning and the present as a provisional end. We attempt to alter the accustomed vision: to see in the present a beginning, in the past an end. This end is also provisional because it changes proportionally as the present changes. If the present is a beginning, the work of Pellicer, Villaurrutia, and Novo is the natural consequence of the work of the young and not the other way around. The youthfulness of these three poets is proved by their acceptance of the proximity of other young poets. The present changes them, grants them new understanding. On the other hand, if there is no living relationship between the present and the past, if the past is oblivious to the acts of the young, there is no risk in affirming that we have broken with the past—such a past does not concern us. I don't wish to say that it is contemptible: it is simply not ours, it does not form a part of our present.

This book is not an anthology but an experiment. It is this in two senses: because of the idea that inspired it and by being a collective work. About the latter I must admit that our concurrence has not been absolute. From the outset certain differences in interpretation have manifested themselves. Nothing is more natural. One of us observed that the idea of "the tradition of severance" is contradictory: if there is tradition, something remains (content or form); the chain is not broken and suddenly dissolved. Another idea is that tradition is preserved, thanks to severance: changes are its continuity. A tradition that immobilizes itself only prolongs death. And more: transmits death. Reply: the example of traditional societies contradicts the supposed virtues brought to life by severance. Nothing changes in them and, nevertheless, the tradition is alive. Rebuttal: the tradition is a modern invention. The so-called traditional peoples do not know that they are that. They repeat inherited gestures outside of history, outside of time—or, better, they are immersed in another age, cyclical and closed. Only severance gives us consciousness of the tradition. New reply: the opposite is what is certain: thanks to the tradition we are made conscious of change. . . . I shall not repeat here all that we said. At one moment in the discussion the real difference came up: Alí Chumacero and José Emilio Pacheco maintained that, on the side of the central criterion of change, we should take into account other values: aesthetic dignity, decorum—in the Horation sense of the word—perfection. Aridjis and I were opposed. It seemed to us that to accept this proposition was to fall back into the eclecticism that for many years dominated the criticism and intellectual life of Mexico. We did not convince them, nor did they convince us. It occurred to me that there remained no other remedy than to publish, in the same book, two selections. New difficulty: some poets would figure in both; however, with different poems. Somebody proposed an intermediate solution: include also authors who cultivate decorum but who, at the same time, concur in the tradition of change. Notwithstanding our wish for a partisan book, Aridjis and I were swayed, unhappily. This explains the presence of names that only in a tangential way pertain to the tradition of change and severance. At the same time we tried when selecting poems to adjust ourselves whenever possible to the idea of mutation. I do not believe that we have been able to do this in all cases. Not important: in spite of the eclecticism of this book, the reader will perceive the continuity of a current that begins with José Juan Tablada, advances and spreads in the work of four or five poets of the following group, later turns away and hides itself—though only to reappear with greater violence in three or four poets of my generation—and, finally, ends up by inspiring most of the new poets.

We divided this book into four parts. The first is dedicated to the young. It is not, nor could it be, a complete selection. More than a picture of recent poetry, it is a window which opens onto a rapidly changing landscape. The second part confronted us with a diverse group whose truly significant work was done not in their youth but in their maturity. It is a generation marked by the Second World War and by the ideological quarrels that preceded it and followed it. Later than the others, as if to recover lost time, it jumped forward toward its youth. We omitted Neftali Beltran and Manuel Ponce because we think that their best work does not correspond to "the tradition of severance." I confess to thinking, though the book was already in the press, that their exclusion was not entirely justified: their case is no different from that of various poets who have been included in this section and in the one following. The third part is more homogeneous. The decisive works of this group, with the exception of José Gorostiza, are those of the young. Someone will fault us for the absence of Jorge Cuesta. His thought profoundly influenced the poets of his generation and those of mine, but his poetry is not in his poems, it is in the work of those fortunate enough to have listened to him. As we bury ourselves in time the names diminish. Therefore it is not strange that the fourth group (1915) includes only four poets. One of those, Alfonso Reyes, does not really belong to the modern tradition, but a limited portion of his work reveals that spirit of adventure and exploration that we are interested in accentuating. The case of López Velarde also seems, at first sight, doubtful. But it is not. Certainly, he is a poet of the tradition: must we be reminded that for him that word (tradition) was synonymous with newness? The third poet of this group is a loner who never published a book of verse: Julio Torri. He was one of the first among us to write prose poems. With him modern humor made its appearance in our language. The fourth poet is a refugee from modernism: José Juan Tablada. He is perhaps our youngest poet.

PREFACE

The preparation of the American edition of this book was not
complicated by any of the considerations Octavio Paz de-
scribes in his introduction. It was complicated by others. The
selection would have to be smaller but representative, the
poems would have to be good but translatable, and they
would have to be poems of interest to American readers,
some of whom would not have ever read a Mexican poem.
Not an impossible job, but not an easy one either. For even
after the selection is made, there is the chance that the trans-
lations may not be very good, that a poet assigned to certain
poems may lose interest in them or find, after having invested
a great deal of time, that he has no sympathy with them. For-
tunately, this happened only infrequently. In selecting trans-
lators I chose poets whose own work I admired and who ex-
pressed an interest in the project; and I did my best to match
up the translator with poems he might find to his taste, at
least partially, if not completely. If their knowledge of Span-
ish was not sufficient for them to translate on their own, they
were provided with a literal version of the original. Most of
them, however, though they were given literal versions, found
they were capable of working the poems out in rough for
themselves, the knowledge of at least one other Romance lan-
guage serving as an aid. This was the case with Donald Jus-
tice, who learned Spanish while translating Villaurrutia, Pel-
licer, and Velarde. In the case of an experienced translator
like W. S. Merwin, no literal version was necessary. And in
the cases of Paul Blackburn and Rachel Benson, who had al-
ready translated certain of the poems I hoped to see included
in this book, I was fortunate to secure permission to reprint
their fine translations.

The reader will notice that this book is not divided into
sections as its Mexican counterpart was. I felt that the drastic
reduction of the book's size would only impair the integrity of
the original divisions. However, the chronological order of
the Mexican book has been preserved.

Of the forty-two poets in the Mexican edition only twenty-four are represented here and, in most cases, by fewer poems. The choice of what poems to include depended on the editor's preference and on the importance of the poet in the original edition. With the exception of Alfonso Reyes, all of the important, amply represented poets in the original book have been retained. The reason Reyes was omitted is that he seems, as Paz indicates in his introduction, somewhat old-fashioned and outside of the "tradition of change." Besides, having appeared some years ago in Samuel Beckett's anthology of Mexican poetry, he is already well known in this country. On the other hand, the editor would like to have included the only poem of Jorge Hernandez Campos that appears in the original edition, but it proved impossible to render adequately into English, and as it is a long poem, its failure would be especially glaring.

The final shape of this book was determined by the quality of the translations. If there were any doubts about the success of the English version, then the poem was scrapped. In the case of poets difficult to render into English—Gilberto Owen, for example—this resulted in severely limited representation. A translation must have the authority of a good poem written in English; this is important because most readers will be reading only the translation and, consciously or unconsciously, they will be using other poems written in English as a standard for judgment. It seemed in the best interests of even those poets represented by just one poem to make the translation the final factor determining inclusion. There did not seem to be any point in having anyone represented by a lot of poorly translated poems. Besides, it was felt that this should be a collection of poems, not poets; that what is being offered the American reader is a view of relatively recent Mexican poetry, not a close look at a handful of poets. It was in this spirit that the American edition was put together.

Mark Strand

ACKNOWLEDGMENTS

I should like to thank Homero and Betty Aridjis for their valuable help in shedding light on certain problems of obscurity in the original poems; and to thank Constance Campbell of The Center for Inter-American Relations for checking over many of the translations, making sure they were free of error, and Suzanne Jill Levine, who prepared the literal versions of many of the poems.

Mark Strand

NEW POETRY
OF MEXICO

HOMERO ARIDJIS
(*nacido en Contepec, Michoacán 1940*)

Ganador de becas del Centro de Escritores Mejicanos y de la Fundación Guggenheim: también es fundador de la revista *Correspondencias*, y es el autor de siete libros de poesía.

A veces uno toca un cuerpo

A veces uno toca un cuerpo y lo despierta
por él pasamos la noche que se abre
la pulsación sensible de los brazos marinos

y como al mar lo amamos
como a un canto desnudo
como al solo verano

Le decimos luz como se dice ahora
le decimos ayer y otras partes

lo llenamos de cuerpos y de cuerpos
de gaviotas que son nuestras gaviotas

Lo vamos escalando punta a punta
con orillas y techos y aldabas

con hoteles y cauces y memorias
y paisajes y tiempo y asteroides

Lo colmamos de nosotros y de alma
de collares de islas y de alma

Lo sentimos vivir y cotidiano
lo sentimos hermoso   pero sombra

HOMERO ARIDJIS
(*born Contepec, Michoacán, 1940*)

Winner of grants from the Mexican Writers Center and the Guggenheim Foundation and founder of the magazine *Correspondencias,* he is the author of several books of poetry.

Sometimes We Touch a Body

Sometimes we touch a body and we wake it
and it is a way through the night which opens
to our senses the pulsing of its arms like the sea's

and we love it like the sea
like a naked song
like the only summer

We say it is light as one says now
we say it is yesterday and other places

we fill it with bodies and bodies
with gulls our own gulls

We go climbing it peak after peak
with ears and roofs and door latches

with hotels and ditches and memories
and landscapes and time and asteroids

We fill it to the brim with ourselves and with soul
with collars of islands and with soul

We feel ourselves living and everyday
we feel ourselves beautiful   but shadow

Translated by W. S. Merwin

24

Es tu nombre y es también octubre

Es tu nombre y es también octubre
es el diván y tus ungüentos
es ella tú la joven de las turbaciones
y son las palomas en vuelos secretos
y el último escalón de la torre
y es la amada acechando el amor en antemuros
y es lo dable en cada movimiento y los objetos
y son los pabellones
y el no estar del todo en una acción
y es el Cantar de los Cantares
y es el amor que te ama
y es un resumen de vigilia
de vigilancia sola al borde de la noche
al borde del soñador y los insomnios
y también es abril y noviembre
y los disturbios interiores de agosto
y es tu desnudez
que absorbe la luz de los espejos
y es tu capacidad de trigo
de hacerte mirar en las cosas
y eres tú y soy yo
y es un caminarte en círculo
dar a tus hechos dimensión de arco
y a solas con tu impulso decirte la palabra

It's Your Name and It's Also October

It's your name and it's also October
it's the bed and your ointments
it's she   you   the young woman whose head's in a whirl
and they're the doves flying in secret
and the last step of the tower
and it's the beloved spying love from the battlements
and it's the consent in each movement and the objects
and they're the pavilions
and the not-being of the all in one act
and it's the Song of Songs
and it's the love that loves you
and it's a sum of watching
of vigilance alone at the edge of the night
at the side of the dreamer and of those who are sleepless
and it's also April and November
and the inner turmoils of August
and it's your nakedness
which the light of the mirrors drinks in
and it's the way you and the wheat have
of showing yourselves in things
and you're you and I'm I
and it's a going around in a circle
to give what you do the dimension of a bow
and alone with your impulse tell you the word

Translated by W. S. Merwin

Antes del reino

Antes del reino
de las aldeas flotantes
de los pies mensajeros
ya eras tú primera sombra
el presagio desatándose
en lenta destrucción de ángeles
ya eras la mano   ya la espada
y el rostro   los dos rostros
y el cinturón que anuda los vientos contrarios

ya eras la ventana última
los ojos últimos
el incendio de luz
la noche sucia
con toses de enferma por las calles

eras tú misma
y tu doble atrás como un espía

Antes del reino
todavía no eras tú
sólo premonición
y ya eras la presencia
la señal como saludo
los cuerpos
la cópula cayéndose a pedazos

Before the Kingdom

Before the kingdom
of the floating villages
of the messenger feet
already you were the first shadow
the foretaste giving rein to itself
in a slow destruction of angels
already you were the hand already the sword
and the face   both faces
and the belt that ties up the rough winds

already you were the last window
the last eyes
the burning of the light
the night befouled
with the coughs of a sick woman in the streets

you were yourself
and your double behind you like a spy

Before the kingdom
you were not yet you
only a premonition
and already you were the presence
the signal like a greeting
the bodies
the copulation falling into fragments

Translated by W. S. Merwin

JOSÉ EMILIO PACHECO
(nacido en Méjico D.F. 1939)

Se mantiene como periodista y editor. Ha publicado dos libros de poesía, *Los elementos de la noche* (1963) y *El reposo del fuego* (1966).

De algún tiempo a esta parte

I

Aquí está el sol con su único ojo, la boca escupefuego que no se hastía de calcinar la eternidad. Aquí está como un rey derrotado que mira desde el trono la dispersión de sus vasallos.

Algunas veces, el pobre sol, el heraldo del día que te afrenta y vulnera, se posaba en su cuerpo, decorando de luz todo lo que fue amado.

Hoy se limita a entrar por la ventana y te avisa que ya han dado las siete y tienes por delante la expiación de tu condena: los papeles que sobrenadan en la oficina, las sonrisas que los otros te escupen, la esperanza, el recuerdo . . . y la palabra: tu enemiga, tu muerte, tus raíces.

II

El día que cumpliste nueve años, levantaste en la playa un castillo de arena. Sus fosos comunicaban con el mar, sus patios hospedaron la reverberación del sol, sus almenas eran incrustaciones de coral y reflejos.

Una legión de extraños se congregó para admirar tu obra. Veías sus panzas comidas por el vello, las piernas de las mujeres, mordidas por cruentas noches y deseos.

Saciado de escuchar que tu castillo era perfecto, volviste a casa, lleno de vanidad. Han pasado doce años desde entonces, y a menudo regresas a la playa, intentas encontrar restos de aquel castillo.

Acusan al flujo y al reflujo de su demolición. Pero no son culpables las mareas: tú sabes que alguien lo abolió a patadas—y que algún día el mar volverá a edificarlo.

III

En el último día del mundo—cuando ya no haya infierno, tiempo ni mañana—dirás su nombre incontaminado de cenizas, de perdones y miedo. Su nombre alto y purísimo, como ese roto instante que la trajo a tu lado.

JOSÉ EMILIO PACHECO
(born in Mexico, D.F., 1939)

Makes his living as a journalist and editor. He has published two books of poetry: *Los Elementos de la Noche* (1963), *El Reposo del Fuego* (1966).

From Some Time to This Place

I

It's the sun with its single eye, the fire-spitting mouth that never tires of charring eternity. Like a broken king who looks from his throne at the rout of his vassals.

Sometimes, the poor sun, the herald of the day who insults and slanders you, settled on your body, adorning with light all you loved.

Today it limits itself to coming in through the window and letting you know that it's already seven o'clock and you still have your sentence to serve: the papers floating in the office, the smiles that others spit on you, hope, memory . . . and the word: your enemy, your death, your origin.

II

The day of your ninth birthday you built a sand castle at the beach. Its moats connected with the sea, its patios lodged the shimmer of the sun, its turrets were incrustations of coral and reflected light.

An army of strangers gathered around to admire your work. You saw their potbellies chewed by curls, the legs of the women gnawed by bloody nights and by desires.

Stuffed with hearing about your perfect castle, you returned home, ripe with conceit. Twelve years have passed since then, and often you return to the beach and try to find the ruins of the castle.

The ebb and flow are blamed for wearing it away. But the tides aren't guilty: you know that someone stamped it down to nothing—and one day the sea will build it again.

III

On the last day of the world—when there is no longer hell, time, or tomorrow—you will say her name uncontaminated by ashes, pardons, and fear. Her name, high and pure, like that split second that brought her to your side.

IV

Suena el mar. La antigua lámpara del alba incendia el pecho de las oscuras islas. El gran buque zozobra, anegado de soledad. Y en la escollera herida por las horas, de pie como un minuto abierto, se demora la noche.

Los seres de la playa tejieron laberintos en el ojo del náufrago, próximo a ser oleaje, fiel rebaño del tiempo. Alga, litoral verde, muchacha destruida que danza y brilla cuando el sol la visita.

V

De algún tiempo a esta parte, las cosas tienen para ti el sabor acre de lo que muere y de lo que comienza. Áspero triunfo de tu misma derrota, viviste cada día con la coraza de la irrealidad. El año enfermo te dejó en rehenes algunas fechas que te cercan y humillan, algunas horas que no volverán pero que viven su confusión en la memoria.

Comenzaste a morir y a darte cuenta de que el misterio no va a extenuarse nunca. El despertar es un bosque de hallazgos, un milagro que recupera lo perdido y que destruye lo ganado. Y el día futuro, una miseria que te encuentra solo: inventando y puliendo tus palabras.

Caminas y prosigues y atraviesas tu historia. Mírate extraño y solo, de algún tiempo a esta parte.

IV

The sea sounds. The old lamp of dawn fires the breast of the dark islands. The great ship founders and drowns in solitude. On the breakwater, wounded by the hours and standing like an open minute, the night takes its time.

The creatures of the shore weaved labyrinths in the eye of the shipwrecked one, on his way to becoming a surge of waves, a flock faithful to time. Algae, green shore, ruined girl who dances and gleams when the sun visits her.

V

From some time to this place, things have for you the sour taste of the dying or beginning. Hard triumph of your own defeat, you lived each day in an armor of illusion. The sick year left as hostages days that enclose and humiliate you, hours that won't come back but still live their confusion in your memory.

You began to die and to realize that the mystery will never be easier. Awakening is a forest of findings, a miracle that finds the lost and destroys the found. And that future day, a misery that finds you alone: inventing and burnishing your words.

Come, chase after and enter your own past. Look at yourself, strange and alone, from some time to this place.

Translated by Philip Levine

La enredadera

Verde o azul, fruto del muro, crece;
divide cielo y tierra.
Con los años
se va haciendo más rígida, más verde,
costumbre de la piedra, cuerpo ávido
de entrelazadas puntas que se tocan,
llevan la misma savia, son una breve planta
y también son un bosque;
son los años
que se anudan y rompen;
son los días
del color del incendio;
son el viento
que a través del otoño
toca el mundo,
las oscuras
raíces de la muerte
y el linaje
de sombra que se alzó en la enredadera.

The Climbing Vine

Green or blue, fruit of the wall, it grows;
separates sky and earth.
With the years it becomes stiffer, greener,
becomes a habit of the stones, an eager body
of interlaced points that touch,
that bear the same sap, are a brief plant
and also a forest;
they are the years
which choke and break;
days
the color of something on fire;
the wind
crossing autumn
to touch the world,
the dark origins of death
and the spawn
of the shadows which rose in the vine.

Translated by Philip Levine

Las palabras de Buda

Todo el mundo está en llamas: lo visible
arde y el ojo en llamas interroga.
Arde el fuego del odio.
                    Arde la usura.
Arden el nacimiento y la caída.
                    Arde el dolor.
El llanto, el sufrimiento
           arden también.
La pesadumbre es llama.
           Y una hoguera es la angustia
en la que arden
        todas las cosas:
Llama,
      arden las llamas,
arden las llamas,
        mundo y fuego, mira
la hoja al viento, tan triste, de la hoguera.

The Words of the Buddha

The whole world is in flames: the visible
burns and the burning eye asks.
The fire of hatred burns.
                  Usury burns.
Birth and the fall burn.
              Pain burns.
Weeping, suffering
            burn also.
The heavy sorrow is a flame.
                  And anguish is a bonfire
in which all things
           burn:
Flame,
      the flames burn,
the flames burn,
           world and fire, look at
the sad leaf in the storm of the bonfire.

Translated by Philip Levine

ÓSCAR OLIVA
(nacido en Tuxtla Gutiérrez, Chiapas 1938)

Actualmente trabaja en el instituto Nacional de Bellas Artes. Ha publicado dos libros de poesía.

Mientras tomo una taza de café . . .

Mientras tomo una taza de café repaso los poemas
que he escrito
¡Cuánta confusión! ¡Cuántas palabras perdidas!
¿Bajo qué impulso lancé mi pecho mis descomposturas
a la búsqueda de ese mar que no es claro ni habitable?
Si he dicho soledad árbol o cieno
fueron palabras imprecisas para extender mis brazos
para darle un vuelco al reloj y mostrar su desnudez
y sus caminos
He tomado conciencia de mis obligaciones
y he querido dar a los hombres nada más un relámpago

Debajo de una imagen ahora me duermo
ahora la doblo ahora la subrayo

Mañana despertaré en un mundo nuevo

ÓSCAR OLIVA
(born Tuxtla Gutiérrez, Chiapas, 1938)

At present works in the Instituto Nacional de Bellas Artes. He has published two books of poetry.

While Drinking a Cup of Coffee . . .

While drinking a cup of coffee I go over the poems I've written
What confusion! What a waste of words!
What prompted my breast to send my disorders
in search of that sea that's neither clear nor habitable?
If I've said solitude tree or mud
they were vague words to stretch my arms
to turn my watch upside down and show its nakedness
and its roads
I've come to realize my obligations
and I've wanted to give men nothing but a flash of lightning

Now I'm sleeping under an image
now I fold it and underline it

Tomorrow I'll wake up in a new world

Translated by W. S. Merwin

FRANCISCO CERVANTES
(*nacido en Querétaro, 1938*)

Periodista de profesión, es además el fundador de la revista *Agora* y también traductor del poeta portugués Fernando Pessoa.

Mambrú

no vino a despedirse
no lo vi
Mambrú se fue a la guerra
qué dolor qué dolor qué pena
no sé cuándo vendrá
de él sólo recuerdo su capa purpúrea
su cabello alejándose con lentitud
detrás su joven paje
más joven que él si esto es posible
fue una tarde fría
pero había sol
¿o el frío sólo lo sentía yo?
pasaron días y días
se fue en silencio
su padre le dijo adiós desde el puente levadizo
su recuerdo su figura eran cada vez más imprecisas
si vendrá para pascua
qué dolor qué dolor qué guasa
o para la trinidad
así vino la pascua
y se llegó la trinidad
La trinidad se acaba
qué dolor qué dolor qué rabia
Mambrú no viene ya
arriba de la torre
el viento parecía cantar
me he subido a la torre

FRANCISCO CERVANTES
(*born Querétaro, 1938*)

A journalist by profession, he is also the founder of the magazine *Agora* and translator of the Portuguese poet Fernando Pessoa.

Mambru

he never came to say good-bye
I never saw him go
Mambru went away to war
what sorrow what sorrow what pain
when will he be home again
I only remember his purple cape
his hair moving slowly away
his young page walking behind
younger than he was if possible
it was a cold afternoon
but it was sunny
or did I only feel the cold?
days passed
he went in silence
his father at the drawbridge said good-bye
his memory his face were less and less clear
will he come home for Easter
what sorrow what sorrow what joy
or for Trinity Sunday
so Easter came
and Trinity Sunday arrived
Trinity Sunday is over
what sorrow what sorrow what anger
Mambru is gone forever
over the tower
the wind seemed to sing
I went up to the tower

qué dolor qué dolor qué corre
do re mi do re fa
para ver si aún vendrá
hasta esta tarde triste
en que he visto venir por el camino
el traje vistoso desgarrado
su lento paso de derrota
por allá viene su paje
qué dolor qué dolor qué traje
do re mi do re fa
qué noticias traerá
entonces recordé
no vino a despedirse
no lo vi.

JAIME AUGUSTO SHELLEY
(*nacido en Méjico D.F. 1937*)

Ganador de una beca del Centro de Escritores Mejicanos. Es un autor de varios libros de poesía.

Los pájaros

Chillaron los pájaros
desorbitando su silencio de altas copas
Descendieron cóndores y cuevos de aceradas plumas
Cientos de voces desencajadas por la ráfaga
tomaron la forma de los árboles y callaron
recuperaron su silencio

Sobreviene el día

what sorrow what sorrow what stairs
do re mi do re fa
hoping to see him from there
until this sad afternoon
when I saw him
come down the road
the fancy uniform all torn
here comes his page
what sorrow what sorrow what rags
do re mi do re fa
what news does he have
then I remembered
he never came to say good-bye
I never saw him go

Translated by Mark Strand

JAIME AUGUSTO SHELLEY
(born Mexico, D.F., 1937)

Winner of a grant from the Mexican Writers Center, he is the author
of several books of poems.

The Birds

The birds shrieked
spilling their high tree-goblet silence
Condors and steel-feathered crows came down
Hundreds of voices shaken loose by the gust of wind
took the form of trees and grew quiet
they regained their silence

Then it is day

Translated by W. S. Merwin

El cerco

Habrá niebla en los tejados
Caerá como nunca sobre largas formas líquidas
  de luna

Tardaremos en llamarle invierno
entretenidos en el grisarse de árboles y cosas
Será—diremos—el tiempo que se viene como otoño
Pero el año se dará redondo y perfecto
como previsto en nuestros viejos libros

Aprendiendo a estar aquí
nos dejaremos llevar los eneros
  por los agostos viernes

Volverá la paz será la lucha
Y en algún corazón recién acariciado
  la espina del tiempo toda

Se harán más viejos los ruidos y la noche
Vendrá el sexo sobre el sexo a fecundar la dicha
Se perderán tus ojos tus palabras
Tomando el cuerpo como mazo
  desearás golpear la tierra que te niega

Será la risa
Será el deseo
La mancha de tu cuerpo
  doblada en las paredes
meando oscuras golondrinas vaporosas
Será la noche que te abrigue
  entre guitarras y hombres en mangas de camisa
dados a no olvidar pequeñas cosas
Será el toque secundado
de alguna campana colmada de sorpresas

The Ring

There will be fog on the roofs
It will fall as never before across broad liquid
   forms of moon

We will be slow to call it winter
delayed by the polishing of trees and things
It will be a season—we say—that ripens like autumn
But the year will grow round and perfect
   as our ancient books predict

Learning to be here
we will let our Januaries be taken from us for August Fridays

Peace will come back it will be conflict
And in some heart caressed not long since
   the thorn of the whole of time

Night and the noises will grow older
Sex will climb upon sex to impregnate fortune
Your eyes your words will be lost
Seizing the body like a mallet
   you'll want to beat on the earth that refuses you

It will be laughter
It will be desire
The stain of your body
   folded on the walls
pissing dark cloudy swallows
It will be the night that shelters you
   among guitars and men in shirt sleeves
reminders of little things
It will be the alto peal
   of some bell tower overflowing with surprises
authorizing the flirting of girls

autorizando el flirt de las muchachas
a la hora del rosario
Será el rostro reluciente del chiquillo
    paseando un caramelo entre los dientes
Habrá ciertamente niebla corriendo
    entre estas torres
y estos pinos perdidos casi en la blancura
Será Xalapa o San Cristóbal
Seremos tiempo anudado a nuestros huesos

at the hour of the rosary
It will be the little boy's face shining
  as he puts a piece of candy between his teeth
There will certainly be fog running
  among these towers
and these pines almost lost in the whiteness
There will be Xalapa or Saint Christopher
We will be time knotted to our bones

Translated by W. S. Merwin

46

SERGIO MONDRAGÓN
(*nacido Cuernavaca* 1935)

Fundador y, conjunto con Margaret Randall, redactor de *El Corno Emplumado*, es al autor del libro de poesía *Yo soy el otro* (1965).

Guru

la melena del león cubre el zoológico del cielo
sus garras se ejercitan en mi pecho que sangra
su cola se mece con suavidad en mis pestañas

es el león de todos los años
de todos los días

es el león del tapiz en el templo
el león blanco con su barba de profeta
y sus ojos mansos sus músculos elásticos

es el león de la Justicia
el león nacido en julio pero que reina en agosto
es el león de las tremendas carcajadas
el león al cual sólo los justos pueden mirar de frente

el león del rugido largo y penetrante
cuyo eco retumba en todos los rincones

la melena del león cae sobre mi frente
y se anida en mi entrecejo
                              mi entrecejo
que sigue aquí cavilando sobre el león
de la Justicia

SERGIO MONDRAGÓN

(*born in Cuernavaca, 1935*)

A founder and coeditor with Margaret Randall of *El Corno Emplumado,* he is the author of one book of poetry: *Yo Soy El Otro* (1965).

Guru

The lion's mane covers the zoo of heaven
his claws practice in my bleeding breast
his tail stirs gently in my eyelashes

he is the lion of all the years
all the days

he is the lion of the temple tapestry
the white lion with his prophet's beard
and his meek eyes his elastic muscles

he is the lion of Justice
the lion born in July who reigns in August
the lion of the tremendous laughs
the lion whom only the just can look in the eye

the lion of the long penetrating roar
whose echo resounds in all the corners

the lion's mane falls across my forehead
and nestles in the space between my eyebrows
                                        the space
that goes on looking hard at the lion
of Justice

Translated by W. S. Merwin

48

GABRIEL ZAID
(*nacido en Monterrey 1934*)

Su ocupación es consultante administrativo. Ha publicado dos libros
de poesía *Fábula de Narciso y Ariadne* y *Seguimiento* (1964).

Nacimiento de Venus

Así surges del agua,
                    blanquísima,
y tus largos cabellos son del mar todavía,
y los vientos te empujan, las olas te conducen,
como el amanecer, por olas, serenísima.
Así llegas helada como el amanecer.
Así la dicha abriga como un manto.

La ofrenda

Mi amada es una tierra agradecida.
Jamás se pierde lo que en ella se siembra.
Toda fe puesta en ella fructifica.
Aun la menor palabra en ella da su fruto.
Todo en ella se cumple, todo llega al verano.
Cargada está de dádivas, pródiga y en sazón.
En sus labios la gracia se siente agradecida.
En sus ojos, su pecho, sus actos, su silencio.
Le he dado lo que es suyo, por eso me lo entrega.
Es el altar, la diosa y el cuerpo de la ofrenda.

GABRIEL ZAID
(*born in Monterrey, 1934*)

Makes his living as a management technician. He has published two books of poetry: *Fabula de Narciso y Ariadne* (1958), *Seguimiento* (1964).

Birth of Venus

Thus you arise from the water,
                                        whitest of all
and your long hair still of the sea,
and you are pressed by the winds, led by the waves
like the dawn, in undulations, most serene.
Thus you arrive, frozen as the dawn.
Thus happiness shelters like a mantle.

Translated by Daniel Hoffman

The Offering

My beloved is a grateful earth.
What's sown in her is never lost.
Placed in her, all faith grows fruitful.
Even the least word in her bears fruit.
All is fulfilled in her, all attains summer.
Laden with gifts she is, prodigal and ripe.
Grace upon her lips feels grateful.
In her eyes, her breasts, her acts, her silence.
To her have I rendered that which is hers.
Therefore to me she returns it.
She is the altar, the goddess, the body of the offering.

Translated by Daniel Hoffman

Pastoral

Una tarde con árboles,
callada y encendida.

Las cosas su silencio
llevan como su esquila.

Tienen sombra: la aceptan.
Tienen nombre: lo olvidan.

Y tú, pastor del Ser,
tú la oveja perdida.

Resplandor último

La luz final que hará
ganado lo perdido.

La luz que va guardando
las ruinas del olvido

La luz con su rebaño
de mármol abatido.

Shepherd's Song

One afternoon with trees
silent and vivid.

Things carry their silence
like a little bell.

They have a shadow, they accept it.
They have a name which they forget.

And thou, pastor of Being,
Thou the lost sheep.

Translated by Daniel Hoffman

Final Splendor

The last light
that will have won the lost.

The light that keeps on guarding
the ruins of oblivion

The light with its flock
of downcast marble.

Translated by Daniel Hoffman

MARCO ANTONIO MONTES DE OCA
(nacido en Méjico D.F. 1932)

Ganador del premio Xavier Villaurrutia en 1959. Es el autor de ocho libros de poesía, entre otros, *Delante de la luz cantan los pájaros* (1959) y *Cantos al sol que no se alcanza* (1961).

La luz en ristre

La creación está de pie,
su espíritu surge entre las blancas dunas
y salpica con hisopos inagotables
los huertos oprimidos por la bota de pedernal
o la fría insolencia de la noche.
Los colores celestes, firmemente posados en los vitrales,
esponjan siluetas de santos;
un resorte de yeso alza sobre el piso miserable
sombras que bracean con angustioso denuedo.
Y llama el cuerno mágico a las creaturas gastadas en el dolor
para que el vértigo maravilloso instaure su hora de resarcimiento
y la ceniza despierte animada en grises borbotones.

La única, espléndida, irresistible creación
está de pie como una osamenta enardecida
y sobrepasa todas las esclusas, toca en cada llama la puerta del in-
    cendio
y ensilla galaxias que un gran mago ha de montar,
cuando el espíritu patrulle por el alba
hasta encontrar los pilares del tiempo vivo.

MARCO ANTONIO MONTES DE OCA
(born Mexico, D.F., 1932)

Winner of the Xavier Villaurrutia prize in 1959, he is the author of
eight books of poetry, among them *Delante de la Luz cantan los pajaros* (1959) and *Cantos al sol que no se alcanza* (1961).

The Light in Its Stand

The creation is on its feet,
its spirit is emerging among the white dunes,
splashing from inexhaustible sprinklers
the fruit gardens crushed by the flint boot
or by the cold insolence of night.
The heavenly colors, held tight in the windows,
beam through the silhouettes of saints;
above the wretched floor
a plaster spring raises shadows that wave
arms in anguish,
reckless. And the magic horn
summons the creatures wasted with suffering
to the marvelous vertigo that brings back their hour of reward
and the ash wakes leaping in torrential grays.

The unique, resplendent, irresistible creation
is on its feet like an impassioned skeleton
and it overflows the sluice gates, in each flame
it touches the door of huge fire
and saddles up galaxies which the great wizard must mount,
when the spirit patrols the dawn
until it comes to the pillars of living time.

Translated by W. S. Merwin

El jardín que los dioses frecuentaron

Extranjera es la luna
en la noche sólo poblada por dos amantes.
Ella y él, en impaciente simulacro,
siegan con el tajo de la vista
las espigas púrpuras de los fuegos de artificio.
Ella y él, de entre el vivac purificado, nacen otra vez,
y vestidos de retama y con el corazón de ambos refundido en uno
    solo,
convocan la sal y acude la blancura.
Ninguna cuña de ajena maravilla cabe
en esa esfera que forman y que no lanza de sí ni un aliento,
pues todo sirve a su robusta plenitud,
todo teje en sus fronteras un suave limbo interior,
una frazada de ser mutuo en la que entibian sus manos
como en fogata de setos de amapolas.
Ahí el amor es ajeno
a la recelosa urdimbre que ganó la niebla
al quehacer del hada
y los joyeles estrangulados con sus propios reflejos
son cada vez menos frecuentes;
ausente está la traición
y si suena contra los juncos
la furia agorera del jabalí, nadie se turba;
pues sólo embiste olvidados racimos de alimañas ya prohibidas,
respetando al fin
el ocio de intensas figuras
con que la luna invade el agua.
Ahí, en esa esfera, en esa pequeña esfera amueblada con lo mejor del
    mundo,
la cabellera de la claridad flagela días nefastos
y al fuego del alma se une
como se unen los dedos al invocar la suerte.
Deslizándose, arqueándose como pantera de aire delicioso
la claridad penetra los moldes terrestres, los nichos,
los hondones sólo visitados por el asesino resplandor de los volcanes.
Y bajo el signo de esta fuente que en la luz se embebe,
el ave se convierte en sollozo y vuela en su propio pecho,

The moon is foreign
in the night peopled only by two lovers.
She and he, impatient image,
harvest, with the blade of sight,
the purple heads of the fireworks.
She and he, from among the purified encampment, are born again,
and dressed in broom and with both hearts melted into one
they call the salt and the whiteness comes.
No wedge of alien wonder fits
into that sphere which they form and which gives off not so much as
    a breath
since everything contributes to its sturdy fullness,
everything weaves on its borders a soft internal limbo,
a blanket of mutual being in which their hands are warmed
as at a blaze of poppy fences.
There love is foreign
to the suspicious warp which the mist won
from the fairy's occupation
and the little jewels strangled with their own reflections
are less and less frequent;
betrayal is absent,
and if the boar's ominous fury sounds
against the rushes, no one is troubled;
for it attacks only forgotten clusters of harmful animals, now out-
    lawed,
respecting, finally,
the leisure of intense figures
with which the moon invades the water.
There in that sphere, in that little sphere furnished with the best that
    is in the world,
the long hair of clarity whips unlucky days
and joins the soul's fire
as fingers join to invoke luck.
Slipping, arching like a panther of delicious air,
clarity penetrates terrestrial molds, niches,
hollows visited only by the murderous splendor of volcanoes.
And under the sign of that fountain from which one drinks while
    there is light
the bird turns into a crying and flies in its own breast,

la memoria llama a los círculos del remolino por su nombre,
y la nieve, heroica como un mortal,
sigue helándose y sobreviviendo
a todos sus males de montaña.
Bajo el signo de la claridad podará el dragón
su renombre de supremo erizo con espinas como torres;
veremos almohadas incendiadas por un beso
y tras el viento coagulado en los vitrales
brillará un puñado de fulgor no mayor que un pájaro,
una lámpara pequeña, solitaria; la esfera de los amantes,
inextinguible como un astro de bolsillo,
prodigiosa como el talismán
que pega los reflejos que quiebro en mi rodilla.

memory calls to the circles of the whirlpool for its name,
and the snow, heroic as a mortal,
goes on freezing and surviving
all its mountain ills.
Under the sign of clarity the dragon will prune
his fame as the great hedgehog with spines like towers;
we will see pillows catch fire at a kiss
and through the wind congealed in the stained glass
a handful of brilliance will shine, no bigger than a bird,
a little solitary lamp; the sphere of the lovers,
inextinguishable, like a pocket star,
prodigious as the talisman
that binds the reflections I break on my knee.

Translated by W. S. Merwin

TOMÁS SEGOVIA
(*nacido en Valencia, 1927*)

Vino a Méjico en 1940 y actualmente reside en Paris. Ensayista, crítica y traductor de poesía (Ungaretti y Rimbaud) ha publicado una novela, una pieza dramática en verso, y cinco libros de poemas, siendo el más reciente *El Sol y Su Eco* en 1960.

La que acoge y conforta

La que acoge y conforta
la que marca con su espera el lugar del término
la que no es pregunta pero hace posible la respuesta verdadera
la que ve mi visión
la que es estela en el agua y oriente en el aire y regazo para ser com-
prendido
la que dialoga en la soledad
la invisible compañía
aquella a quien hablan las palabras no dichas
la que vive y respira en mi intención
la que recibe mis pensamientos
la que devuelve mis preguntas transfiguradas
la aguja del compás cuya punta errante soy yo
la que hace mi casa en todas partes
la que conversa en el bosque que oigo hablar
la que medita en el crepúsculo que me inunda
la que duerme en los soplos que me hablan
la que ríe siempre ríe en el día inmortal
ella
horizonte que mira luz que acaricia
medida del cambio alma del vuelo
secreto del amor
—traicionada olvidada perdida
ángel negada mirada sin respuesta
reina desfigurada diosa muda
el viento ya no es tu voz
mis horas no son las perlas que tu mirada traspasa y une
mis palabras se disuelven en el aire
ya no sé descifrar lo que digo lo que hago
alguien que no he llamado se instala en mí y piensa brutalmente
su mirada feroz nunca se tranquiliza

(born in Valencia, 1927)

Came to Mexico in 1940 and now lives in Paris. Essayist, critic, and
translator of poetry (Ungaretti and Rimbaud). He has published a
novel, a verse play, and five books of poems, the most recent being *El
Sol y Su Eco* (1960).

What Welcomes and Comforts

What welcomes and comforts
what marks the final place with its waiting
what is not a question but makes the right answer possible
what my vision sees
what is in water a wake and in air a source and open to
    understanding
what carries on a dialogue in seclusion
the invisible company
to whom unspoken words speak
what lives and breathes in my purpose
what receives my thoughts
what returns my questions transfigured
the compass needle whose wrong point I am
what turns everywhere into my house
what converses in the woods that I hear speaking
what meditates in the twilight that drowns me
what sleeps in gusts that speak to me
what laughed always laughed in the immortal day
she
horizon that looks light that fondles
measure of change soul of flight
secret of love
—traitor forgotten lost
forbidden angel looked at giving back nothing
disfigured queen mute goddess
the wind is no longer your voice
my hours are not pearls that your stare transfixes and joins
my words dissolve in air
I do not know how to interpret what I say what I do
someone I did not ask for set himself up in me and thinks ferociously
his wild look never lets up

y el agua no tiene alma el aire no palpita
la tierra está gris y yerta como un asesinado
nada canta nada ríe el coro está disperso
el tiempo suena a hueco las horas caen a tropezones
qué espero por qué vivo
por qué cierro los ojos con violencia en espera de que acabe el día
quién es este que se obstina en ofrecerse al torrente del tiempo
por qué pisa la tierra por qué respira el aire
por qué mancha y aplasta y pudre en torno suyo
ah no permitas más esta vergüenza
ángel alma pureza ven
vuelve no te lleves la espada de fuego
incéndiame lléname hasta los bordes de pesada ceniza
sacúdeme con tu vuelo huracanado
no me perdones no soy yo a quien perdonas en mí
devuélveme tu amor y tu desgarradora exigencia
tu dura alegría tu quemadura solar
cuando fui el amado de la tierra desnuda
el deseado de la pulcra indigencia
el predilecto de la Madre descarnada
cómo podré perder la culpa de perderte
matar el asesinato borrar la ausencia
olvidar el olvido apartar este desvío
cómo llamarte sin violar el secreto de tu nombre
cómo pedirte una respuesta a ti silencio suficiente
una sola palabra proferida paralizaría coagularía pulverizaría tu amor
cómo buscarte sin apartar los ojos de este horror
no no te miro no tienes que mostrarte no digas nada
mas sigue detrás de mí materna Eurídice.

and water has no soul air does not flutter
the earth is gray and stiff as a corpse
nothing sings nothing laughs the choir is scattered
time sleeps the hours stumble into a hole
what do I hope for why do I live
why do I shut my eyes violently hoping to finish the day
who is this so bent on offering himself to the rush of time
why tread the earth why breathe the air
why soil and flatten and corrupt everything around oneself
oh put an end to this confusion
angel pure soul come
come back and bring your flaming sword
set me on fire fill me with heavy ash
shake me with your stormy flight
do not forgive me I am not the one you forgive in me
give me back your love and your heartbreaking demands
your hard joy your burned-down plot
when I was the love of that naked earth
the one beautiful indigence longed for
the darling of the lean Mother
how shall I rid myself of the guilt of losing you
to kill treachery to erase absence
to forget forgetfulness to divide this division
how can I call you without violating the secret of your name
how can I ask you to answer your fitting silence
just one word uttered would paralyze clot grind down your love
how can I look for you without taking my eyes from all this horror
no no I don't look at you you don't have to show yourself or say
   anything
just stay with me maternal Eurydice.

Translated by Mark Strand

JAIME SABINES
(nacido en Tuxtla Gutiérrez, Chiapas 1925)

Un hombre de negocios, ha publicado cinco libros de poesía.

Yo no lo sé de cierto . . .

Yo no lo sé de cierto, pero lo supongo
que una mujer y un hombre
algún día se quieren,
se van quedando solos poco a poco,
algo en su corazón les dice que están solos,
solos sobre la tierra se penetran,
se van matando el uno al otro.

Todo se hace en silencio. Como
se hace la luz dentro del ojo.
El amor une cuerpos.
En silencio se van llenando el uno al otro.

Cualquier día despiertan, sobre brazos;
piensan entonces que lo saben todo.
Se ven desnudos y lo saben todo.

(Yo no lo sé de cierto. Lo supongo.)

JAIME SABINES
(born in Tuxtla Gutiérrez, Chiapas, 1925)

Makes his living as a businessman. He has published five books of poetry.

I Don't Know for Certain . . .

I don't know for certain but I suppose
that one day a man and a woman
love each other,
and little by little they become alone,
something in their heart tells them that they're alone,
alone on the earth penetrating each other,
killing each other.

It all happens in silence. The way
light is made in the eye.
Love unites bodies.
They fill each other with silence.

One day they wake up, above arms;
then they think they know it all.
They see themselves naked and they know it all.

(I don't know it for certain. I suppose it.)

Translated by W. S. Merwin

Tarumba

Tarumba.
Yo voy con las hormigas
entre las patas de las moscas.
Yo voy con el suelo, por el viento,
en los zapatos de los hombres,
en las pezuñas, las hojas, los papeles;
voy a donde vas, Tarumba,
de donde vienes, vengo.
Conozco a la araña.
Sé eso que tú sabes de ti mismo
y lo que supo tu padre.
Sé lo que me has dicho de mí.
Tengo miedo de no saber,
de estar aquí como mi abuela
mirando la pared, bien muerta.
Quiero ir a orinar a la luz de la luna.
Tarumba, parece que va a llover.

A la casa del día

A la casa del día entran gentes y cosas,
yerbas de mal olor,
caballos desvelados,
aires con música,
maniquíes iguales a muchachas;
entramos tú, Tarumba, y yo.
Entra la danza. Entra el sol.
Un agente de seguros de vida
y un poeta.
Un policía.
Todos vamos a vendernos, Tarumba.

Tarumba

Tarumba.
I go with the ants
among the feet of the flies.
I go with the ground, through the wind,
in the shoes of men,
in the cloven hooves, the leaves, the papers;
I go where you go, Tarumba,
where you come from, I'm coming.
I know the spider.
I know what you know of yourself
and what your father knew.
I know what you've told me of me.
I'm afraid not to know,
to be here like my grandmother
looking at the wall, good and dead.
I want to go out and piss in the moonlight.
Tarumba, it looks like rain.

Translated by W. S. Merwin

In the House of the Day

People and things enter the house of the day,
stinkweeds,
the horses of insomnia,
catchy tunes,
window dummies that are girls;
you and I enter, Tarumba.
The dance enters. The sun enters.
An insurance agent enters
and a poet.
A cop.
We're all going to sell ourselves, Tarumba.

Translated by Philip Levine

A caballo

A caballo, Tarumba,
hay que montar a caballo
para recorrer este país,
para conocer a tu mujer,
para desear a la que deseas,
para abrir el hoyo de tu muerte,
para levantar tu resurrección.
A caballo tus ojos,
el salmo de tus ojos,
el sueño de tus piernas cansadas.
A caballo en el territorio de la malaria,
tiempo enfermo,
hembra caliente,
risa a gotas.
A donde llegan noticias de vírgenes,
periódicos con santos,
y telegramas de corazones deportivos como una bandera.
A caballo, Tarumba, sobre el río,
sobre la laja de agua, la vigilia,
la hoja frágil del sueño
(cuando tus manos se despiertan con nalgas),
y el vidrio de la muerte en el que miras
tu corazón pequeño.
A caballo, Tarumba,
hasta el vertedero del sol.

On Horseback

On horseback, Tarumba,
you've got to ride a horse
to cover this ground,
to know your woman,
to want the one you want,
to open the hole of your death,
to get your resurrection off the ground.
On horseback your eyes,
the psalm of your eyes,
the sleep in your tired legs.
On horseback in the malarial lands,
sick time,
hot woman,
drops of laughter.
Where news of virgins arrives,
newspapers with saints,
and telegrams of sporting hearts like banners.
On horseback, Tarumba, over the river,
over the flat stones of water, the vigil,
the fragile leaf of sleep,
(when your hands waken around an ass)
and the mirror of death in which you see
your little heart.
On horseback, Tarumba,
as far as the sinkhole of the sun.

Translated by Philip Levine

Si alguien te dice que no es cierto

Si alguien te dice que no es cierto,
dile que venga,
que ponga sus manos sobre su estómago y jure,
que atestigue la verdad de todo.
Que mire la luz en el petróleo de la calle,
los automóviles inmóviles,
las gentes pasando y pasando,
las cuatro puertas que dan al este,
las bicicletas sin nadie,
los ladrillos, la cal amorosa,
las estanterías a tu espalda cayéndose,
las canas en la cabeza de tu padre,
el hijo que no tiene tu mujer,
y el dinero que entra con la boca llena de mierda.
Díle que jure, en el nombre de Dios invicto
en el torneo de las democracias,
haber visto y oído.
Porque ha de oír también el crimen de los gatos
y un enorme reloj al que dan cuerda pegado a tu oreja.

If Someone Tells You It's Not for Sure

If someone tells you it's not for sure,
tell him to come here,
to put his hands over his stomach and swear,
to bear witness to the whole truth.
To see the light in the oily street,
the stopped cars,
the people passing and passing,
the four doors which face the East,
the empty bicycles,
the bricks, the affectionate quicklime,
the bookshelves tumbling behind you,
the gray hairs on your father's head,
the son your wife never had,
and the money that walks in with its mouth full of shit.
In the name of the undefeated God
in the contest of the democracies,
tell him to swear he's seen and heard.
Because he's also got to hear the crime of the cats
and keep his ears glued to the big clock they keep winding.

Translated by Philip Levine

Te puse una cabeza

Te puse una cabeza sobre el hombro
y empezó a reír;
una bombilla eléctrica,
y se encendió.
Te puse una cebolla
y se arrimó un conejo.
Te puse mi mano
y estallaste.

Di cuatro golpes sobre tu puerta
a las doce de la noche
con el anillo lunar,
y me abrió la sábana que tiene cuerpo de mujer,
y entré a lo oscuro.

En el agua estabas como una serpiente
y tus ojos brillaban con el verde que les corresponde a esas horas.
Entró el viento conmigo
y le subió la falda a la delicia, que se quedó inmóvil.
El reloj empezó a dar la una
de cuarto en cuarto, con una vela en la mano.
La araña abuelita tejía
y la novia del gato esperaba a su novio.
Afuera, Dios roncaba.
Y su vara de justicia, en manos del miedo ladrón
dirigía un vals en la orquesta.
Me soplaste en el ombligo
y me hinché y ascendí entre los ángeles.
Pero tuve tiempo de ponerme la camisita
y los zapatitos con que me bautizaron.
Tú quedaste como un cigarro ardiendo en el suelo.

I Put a Head

I put a head on your shoulders
and it started to laugh,
a bulb,
and it lit up.
I put an onion,
and a rabbit drew near,
I put my hand on you
and you went off.

At midnight
I knocked four times on your door
with the ring around the moon,
and the sheet with a woman's body opened
and I entered the darkness.

In the water you were like a serpent
and your eyes glittered with the right green for those hours.
The wind entered with me
and went up your skirt right to the joy, that didn't even move.
Holding a candle, the clock began to strike one
from room to room.
Grandmother spider weaved
and the cat's girl waited for her sweetheart.
Outside God snored.
And in the hands of fear, the thief, His rod of justice
led the orchestra in a waltz.
You breathed into my navel
and I puffed up and ascended among the angels.
But I had time to put on my little shirt
and the shoes in which they baptized me.
You stayed on the ground smoldering like a cigarette.

Translated by Philip Levine

Vamos a cantar

Vamos a cantar:
tararí, tatá.
El viejito cojo
se duerme con sólo un ojo.
El viejito manco
duerme trepado en un zanco.
Tararí, totó.
No me diga nada usted:
se empieza a dormir mi pie.
Voy a subirlo a mi cuna
antes que venga la tía Luna.
Tararí, tui,
tui.

He aquí que estamos reunidos

He aquí que estamos reunidos
en esta casa como en el Arca de Noé:
Blanca, Irene, María y otras muchachas,
Jorge, Eliseo, Óscar, Rafael . . .
Vamos a conocernos rápidamente
y a fornicar y a olvidarnos.
El buey, el tigre, la paloma, el lagarto y el asno, todos
juntos bebemos, y nos pisamos y nos atropellamos
en esta hora que va a hundirse en el diluvio nocturno.
Relámpagos de alcohol cortan la oscuridad de las pupilas
y los truenos y la música se golpean entre las voces desnudas.
Gira la casa y navega hacia las horas altas.
¿Quién te tiene la mano, Magdalena, hundida en las almohadas?
¡Qué bello oficio el tuyo, de desvestirte
y alumbrar la sala!
¡Haz el amor, paloma, con todo lo que sabes:
tus entrenadas manos, tu boca, tus ojos,
tu corazón experto!

Let's Sing

Let's sing:
tarrara, boom da.
Little old gimper
falls asleep with one eye.
Little old one-arm
snoozes perched on a stilt.
Rarrara, boom boo.
Don't tell me nothing:
my foot begins to drowse.
I'm going to lug it up to my cradle
before Auntie Moon gets here.
Tarrara, boom di,
boom, di.

Translated by Philip Levine

So Here We Are

So here we are together
in this house like in Noah's Ark:
Blanca, Irene, Maria, and the other girls,
Jorge, Eliseo, Oscar, Rafael . . .
Let's get down right away
and fuck and forget each other.
The ox, the tiger, the dove, the lizard, and the jackass, all of us
booze together, and knock each other over and rush to it
in this hour about to sink into the night flood.
Bolts of alcohol slice the darkness of the pupils
and the thunder and the music storm each other among the naked
     voices.
The house spins and sails toward the small hours.
Collapsed in the pillows, Magdalena, who holds your hand?
What a beautiful job you do, undressing yourself
and lighting up the room!
Keep loving, baby, with everything you know:
your trained hands, your mouth, your eyes,
your professional heart!

He aquí la cabeza del día, Salomé,
para que bailes delante de todos los ojos en llamas.
¡Cuidado, Lesbia, no nos quites ni un pétalo de las manos!
Sube en el remolino la casa y el tiempo sube
como la harina agria. ¡Hénos aquí a todos, fermentados,
brotándonos por todo el cuerpo el alma!

Algo sobre la muerte del mayor Sabines

I

Mientras los niños crecen, tú, con todos los muertos
poco a poco te acabas.
Yo te he ido mirando a través de las noches
por encima del mármol, en tu pequeña casa.
Un día ya sin ojos, sin nariz, sin orejas,
otro día sin garganta,
la piel sobre tu frente, agrietándose, hundiéndose,
tronchando oscuramente el trigal de tus canas.
Todo tú sumergido en humedad y gases
haciendo tus deshechos, tu desorden, tu alma,
cada vez más igual tu carne que tu traje,
más madera tus huesos y más huesos las tablas.
Tierra mojada donde había una boca,
aire podrido, luz aniquilada,
el silencio tendido a todo tu tamaño
germinando burbujas bajo las hojas de agua.
(Flores dominicales a dos metros arriba
te quieren pasar besos y no te pasan nada.)

II

Mientras los niños crecen y las horas nos hablan,
tú, subterráneamente, lentamente, te apagas.
Lumbre enterrada y sola, pabilo de la sombra,
veta de horror para el que te escarba.

¡Es tan fácil decirte "padre mío"
y es tan difícil encontrarte, larva
de Dios, semilla de esperanza!
Quiero llorar a veces, y no quiero

Here's the head of the day, Salome,
so you can dance before all our eyes on fire.
Careful, Lesbia, don't take one petal from our hands!
The house rises in the whirlwind and time rises
like sourdough. Here we are, all of us, fermenting,
our souls growing out all over our bodies.

Translated by Philip Levine

Something on the Death of the Eldest Sabines

I.

Little by little, while the children grow,
you, with all the dead, are finishing.
Across the nights, I've been looking at you
over the marble, in your little house.
One day without eyes, nose, ears,
another day without your throat,
the skin over your forehead collapsing, sinking,
darkly breaking off in the wheat field of your gray hairs.
All of you submerged in humidity and gases,
going about your undoing, your disorder, your soul,
more and more your flesh and your suit becoming one,
your bones more wooden, and your wooden world more bony.
Where there was a mouth, wet earth,
bad air, annihilated light,
a measure of silence laid out over you
and breeding bubbles under the leaves of water.
(Six feet above, the Sunday flowers
want to pass down kisses and pass nothing.)

II.

While the children grow and the hours talk to us,
underground you slowly go out.
Alone and buried light, wick of the darkness,
vein of horror for whoever unearths you.

It's so hard to say, "My father,"
and so hard to find you, larva
of God, seed of hope!
Sometimes I want to cry, and I don't want

llorar porque me pasas
como un derrumbe, porque pasas
como un viento tremendo, como un escalofrío
debajo de las sábanas,
como un gusano lento a lo largo del alma.
¡Si sólo se pudiera decir: "Papá, cebolla,
polvo, cansancio, nada, nada, nada"!
¡Si con un trago se tragara!
¡Si con este dolor te apuñalara!
¡Si con este desvelo de memorias
—herida abierta, vómito de sangre—
te agarrara la cara!
Yo sé que tú ni yo,
ni un par de valvas,
ni un becerro de cobre, ni unas alas
sosteniendo la muerte, ni la espuma
en que naufraga el mar, ni—no—las playas,
la arena, la sumisa piedra con viento y agua
ni el árbol que es abuelo de su sombra,
ni nuestro sol, hijastro de sus ramas,
ni la fruta madura, incandescente,
ni la raíz de perlas y de escamas,
ni tu tío, ni tu chozno, ni tu hipo,
ni mi locura, y ni tus espaldas,
sabrán del tiempo oscuro que nos corre
desde las venas tibias a las canas.

(Tiempo vacío, ampolla de vinagre,
caracol recordando la resaca.)
He aquí que todo viene, todo pasa,
todo, todo se acaba.
¿Pero tú? ¿pero yo? ¿pero nosotros?
¿para qué levantamos la palabra?
¿de qué sirvió el amor?
¿cuál era la muralla
que detenía la muerte? ¿dónde estaba
el niño negro de tu guarda?
Ángeles degollados puse al pie de tu caja,
y te eché encima tierra, piedras, lágrimas,
para que ya no salgas, para que no salgas.

to because you enter me
like a landslide, because you enter
like a tremendous wind, like a chill
under the covers,
like a slow worm along the length of my soul.
If only I could say: "Papa, onion,
dust, weariness, nothing, nothing, nothing!"
If I could swallow you with one gulp.
If I could stab you with this ache.
If in this sleeplessness of memories
—opened wound, vomit of blood—
I could hold on to your face!
I know that neither you nor I,
nor a pair of valves,
nor a copper calf, nor those wings
upholding death, nor the foam
in which the sea is wrecked, —no—nor the beaches,
the sand, the stones humbled by wind and water,
nor the tree that is grandfather of its shadow,
nor our sun, stepchild of the branches,
nor ripe and incandescent fruit,
nor its roots of pearls and fish scales,
nor your uncle, nor your great-grandson, nor your belch,
nor my madness, nor your shoulders,
will know of the dark time that races through us
from the lukewarm veins to the gray hairs.

(Empty time, blister of vinegar,
snail recalling the undertow.)
Here, everything comes, everything passes,
everything, everything ends.
But you? but I? but us?
why did we lift up the word?
what good was love?
which wall
held back death? where was
the black child who guarded you?
I put decapitated angels at the foot of your coffin,
and I threw earth, stones, tears on you,
so that you won't leave, so that you won't leave.

Translated by Philip Levine

JAIME GARCÍA TERRÉS
(*nacido en Méjico D.F. 1924*)

El embajador actual en Grecia, ha publicado dos libros de poesía y
varios volúmenes de ensayos.

Ipanema

El mar es una historia
que llevo entre los ojos y la sombra
de mis ojos, desleída
ya por los años y sin brío.

Ya se me escapan
sus ecos mal nacidos, sus lugares
de gruesa burla. Pero todavía
llueve la tarde en Ipanema,
a través de los años,
                    contra mis pupilas:
llueven copos de sol. Y se desgajan
en un débil combate las hileras de casas.

JAIME GARCÍA TERRÉS
(born Mexico, D.F., 1924)

Currently ambassador to Greece, he has published two books of poems and several volumes of essays.

Ipanema

The sea is a story
which I carry between my eyes and the shadow
of my eyes, dissolved now
by the years, faint.

By now its abortive echoes
elude me, the settings
of its coarse jokes. But it's still raining
in the afternoon, in Ipanema,
through the years,
                    against my eyelids:
bundles of sunlight are raining. And in
a feeble struggle the lines of the houses are broken.

Translated by W. S. Merwin

JUAN JOSÉ ARREOLA
(nacido en Ciudad Guzmán, Jalisco 1918)

Estudió drama con Rodolfo Usigli y Xavier Villaurrutia, fué uno de los dos fundadores de la revista *Pan*. Ha publicado varios libros de poesía entre ellos *Confabulario total*.

Elegía

Esas que allí se ven, vagas cicatrices entre los campos de labor, son las ruinas del campamento de Nobílior. Más allá se alzan los emplazamientos militares de Castillejo, de Renieblas y de Peña Redonda . . . De la remota ciudad sólo ha quedado una colina cargada de silencio. Y junto a ella, bordeándola, esa ruina de río. El arroyo Merdancho musita su cantilena de juglar, y sólo en las crecidas de junio resuena con épica grandeza.

Esta llanura apacible vio el desfile de los generales ineptos. Nobílior, Lépido, Furio Filo, Cayo Hostilio Mancino . . . Y entre ellos el poeta Lucilio, que paseó aquí con aires de conquistador, y que volvió a Roma maltrecho y abatido, caídas la espada y la lira, boto ya el fino dardo de su epigrama.

Legiones y legiones se estrellaron contra los muros invencibles. Millares de soldados cayeron ante las flechas, el desaliento y el invierno. Hasta que un día el exasperado Escipión se alzó en el horizonte como una ola vengativa, y apretó con sus manos tenaces, sin soltar durante meses, el duro pescuezo de Numancia.

La caverna

Nada más que horror, espacio puro y vacío. Eso es la caverna de Tribenciano. Un hueco de piedra en las entrañas de la tierra. Una cavidad larga y redondeada como un huevo. Doscientos metros de largo, ochenta de anchura. Cúpula por todas partes, de piedra jaspeada y lisa.

Se baja a la caverna por setenta escalones, practicados en tramos desiguales, a través de una grieta natural que se abre como un simple boquete a ras del suelo. ¿Se baja a qué? Se bajaba a morir. En todo

JUAN JOSÉ ARREOLA
(born Ciudad Guzman, Jalisco, 1918)

Studied drama with Rodolfo Usigli and Xavier Villaurrutia, was a co-founder of the magazine *Pan*. He has published several books of poetry, among them *Confabulario Total* (1962).

Elegy

Those vague scars that can be seen there among the plowed fields are the ruins of the camp of Nobilior. Farther on rise the military positions of Castillejo, Renieblas, and Peña Redonda . . .
Nothing is left of the distant city except one hill heavy with silence. And next to it, running beside it, that ruin of a river. The little stream Merdancho hums its ballad refrain, and resounds with epic greatness only in the sudden flash floods of June.
This tranquil plain witnessed the succession of incompetent generals. Nobilior, Lepidus, Furious Filus, Caius Hostilius Mancinus. . . . And among them the poet Lucilius, who sauntered here with the airs of a conqueror, and returned to Rome ill used and beaten, his sword and his lyre both dragging, and his sharp tongue blunted.
Legions upon legions were shattered against those invincible walls. Thousands of soldiers went down under the arrows, despair, the winter. Until one day the enraged Scipio loomed upon the horizon like an avenging wave and seized in his unyielding hands the tough neck of Numancia, month after month without letting go.

Translated by W. S. Merwin

The Cave

Nothing but horror, pure and empty. That is the cave of Tribenciano. A stone void in the bowels of the earth. A cavity, long and rounded like an egg. Two hundred meters long, eighty wide. A dome in every direction, of marbled smooth stone.
There are seventy steps going down to the cave, arranged in flights of different lengths along a natural fissure that opens like an ordinary crack in the ground. What does one go down to? At one time it was

el piso de la caverna hay huesos, y mucho polvo de huesos. No se sabe si las víctimas ignotas bajaban por iniciativa propia, o eran enviadas allí por mandato especial. ¿De quién? Algunos investigadores piensan que la caverna no entraña un misterio cruento. Dicen que se trata de un antiguo cementerio, tal vez etrusco, tal vez ligur. Pero nadie puede permanecer en la espelunca por más de cinco minutos, a riesgo de perder totalmente la cabeza. Los hombres de ciencia quieren explicar el desmayo que sufren los que en ella se aventuran, diciendo que a la caverna afloran subterráneas emanaciones de gas. Pero nadie sabe de qué gas se trata ni por dónde sale. Tal vez lo que allí ataca al hombre es el horror al espacio puro, la nada en su cóncava mudez. No se sabe más acerca de la caverna de Tribenciano. Miles de metros cúbicos de nada, en su redondo autoclave. La nada en cáscara de piedra. Piedra jaspeada y lisa. Con polvo de muerte.

Telemaquia

Dondequiera que haya un duelo, estaré de parte del que cae. Ya se trate de héroes o rufianes.

Estoy atado por el cuello a la teoría de esclavos esculpidos en la más antigua de las estelas. Soy el guerrero moribundo bajo el carro de Asurbanipal, y el hueso calcinado en los hornos de Dachau.

Héctor y Menelao, Francia y Alemania y los dos borrachos que se rompen el hocico en la taberna me abruman con su discordia. Adondequiera que vuelvo los ojos, me tapa el paisaje del mundo un inmenso paño de Verónica con el rostro del Bien Escarnecido.

Espectador a la fuerza, veo a los contendientes que inician la lucha y quiero estar de parte de ninguno. Porque yo también soy dos: el que pega y el que recibe las bofetadas.

El hombre contra el hombre. ¿Alguien quiere apostar?

Señoras y señores: No hay salvación. En nosotros se está perdiendo la partida. El Diablo juega ahora con las piezas blancas.

to die. There are bones on the cave floor, and quantities of bone dust. No one knows whether the nameless victims went down of their own free will or were sent there by some special order. And whose?

Some students of the cave are convinced that it is not the abode of any cruel mystery. They say that it all has to do with an ancient cemetery, perhaps Etruscan, perhaps Ligurian. But no one can remain in that cavern for more than five minutes: he runs the risk of completely losing his mind.

Men of science prefer to explain the fainting that overcomes those who venture inside by saying that underground gas leaks seep into the cave. But no one knows what kind of gas it might be nor where it comes from. It may be that what seizes a man there is the horror of pure space: nothing, in its concave muteness.

No more is known about the cave of Tribenciano. Thousands of cubic meters of nothing in its round pot. Nothing, in a rind of stone. Marbled smooth stone. Holding death dust.

Translated by W. S. Merwin

Telemachus

Wherever there's a fight I'll be on the side that falls. Now it's heroes or thugs.

I'm tied by the neck to the slave concept carved on the oldest standing stones. I'm the dying warrior under Assurbanipal's chariot, and the calcined bone in the ovens of Dachau.

Hector and Menelaus, France and Germany, and the two drunks who push in each others' faces in the bar wear me out with their disputes. Wherever I turn my eyes the landscape of the world is hidden by an enormous Veronica's Veil showing the face of the Despised Good.

I the observer of force see which of the combatants starts the fight, and I want to be on no one's side. Because I also am two: the one who strikes and the one who receives the blows.

Man against man. Any bets?

Ladies and gentlemen, there is no salvation. The game is being lost within ourselves. At this moment the Devil's playing with the white pieces.

Translated by W. S. Merwin

El sapo

Salta de vez en cuando, sólo para comprobar su radical estático. El salto tiene algo de latido: viéndolo bien, el sapo es todo corazón. Prensado en un bloque de lodo frío, el sapo se sumerge en el invierno como una lamentable crisálida. Se despierta en primavera, consciente de que ninguna metamorfosis se ha operado en él. Es más sapo que nunca, en su profunda desecación. Aguarda en silencio las primeras lluvias.

Y un buen día surge de la tierra blanda, pesado de humedad, henchido de savia rencorosa, como un corazón tirado al suelo. En su actitud de esfinge hay una secreta proposición de canje, y la fealdad del sapo aparece ante nosotros con una abrumadora cualidad de espejo.

Cérvidos

Fuera del espacio y del tiempo, los ciervos discurren con veloz lentitud y nadie sabe dónde se ubican mejor, si en la inmovilidad o en el movimiento que ellos combinan de tal modo que nos vemos obligados a situarlos en lo eterno.

Inertes o dinámicos, modifican continuamente el ámbito natural y perfeccionan nuestras ideas acerca del tiempo, el espacio y la traslación de los móviles. Hechos a propósito para solventar la antigua paradoja, son a un tiempo Aquiles y la tortuga, el arco y la flecha: corren sin alcanzarse; se paran y algo queda siempre fuera de ellos galopando.

El ciervo, que no puede estarse quieto, avanza como una aparición, ya sea entre los árboles reales o desde un boscaje de leyenda: Venado de San Huberto que lleva una cruz entre los cuernos o cierva que amamanta a Genoveva de Brabante. Donde quiera que se encuentren, el macho y la hembra componen la misma pareja fabulosa.

Pieza venatoria por excelencia, todos tenemos la intención de cobrarla, aunque sea con la mirada. Y si Juan de Yepes nos dice que fue tan alto, tan alto que le dio a la caza alcance, no se está refiriendo a la paloma terrenal sino al ciervo profundo, inalcanzable y volador.

The Toad

Every so often he jumps, just to make it clear that he is essentially immobile. The jump is in some way like a heartbeat: careful observation makes it plain that the whole of the toad is a heart.

Clamped in hunk of cold mud, the toad sinks into the winter like a mournful chrysalis. He wakes in the spring knowing that he has not changed into anything else. Dried to his depths, he is more a toad than ever. He waits in silence for the first rains.

And one fine day he heaves himself out of the pliant earth, heavy with moisture, swollen with spiteful sap, like a heart tossed onto the ground. In his sphinxlike posture there is a secret proposition of exchange, and the toad's ugliness appals us like a mirror.

Translated by W. S. Merwin

Deer

Outside space and time, the deer wander, at once swift and languid, and no one knows whether their true place is in immobility or in movement; they combine the two in such a way that we are forced to place them in eternity.

Inert or dynamic, they keep changing the natural horizon, and they perfect our ideas of time, space, and the laws of moving bodies. Made expressly to solve the ancient paradox, they are at once Achilles and the tortoise, the bow and the arrow. They run without ever overtaking. They stop and something remains always outside them, galloping.

The deer cannot stand still, but moves forward like an apparition, whether it be among real trees or out of a grove in a legend: Saint Hubert's Stag bearing a cross between his antlers, or the doe that gives suck to Genevieve of Brabant. Wherever they are met, the male and the female comprise the same fabulous pair.

Quarry without peer, all of us mean to take it, even if only with the eyes. And if Juan de Yepes tells us that what he pursued, when hunting, was so high, so high—he is not referring to the earthly dove, but to the deer: profound, unattainable, and in flight.

Translated by W. S. Merwin

Metamorfosis

Como un meteoro capaz de resplandecer con luz propia a mediodía, como un joyel que contradice de golpe a todas las moscas de la tierra que cayeron en un plato de sopa, la mariposa entró por la ventana y fue a naufragar directamente en el caldillo de lentejas.

Deslumbrado por su fulgor instantáneo (luego disperso en la superficie grasienta de la comida grasera), el hombre abandonó su rutina alimenticia y se puso inmediatamente a restaurar el prodigio. Con paciencia maniática recogió una por una las escamas de aquel tejado infinitesimal, reconstruyó de memoria el dibujo de las alas superiores e inferiores, devolviendo su gracia primitiva a las antenas y a las patitas, vaciando y rellenando el abdomen hasta conseguir la cintura de avispa que lo separa del tórax, eliminando cuidadosamente en cada partícula preciosa los más ínfimos residuos de manteca, desdoro y humedad.

La sopa y la vida conyugal se enfriaron definitivamente. Al final de la tarea, que consumió los mejores años de su edad, el hombre supo con angustia que había disecado un ejemplar de mariposa común y corriente, una *Aphrodita vulgaris maculata* de esas que se encuentran a millares, clavadas con alfileres, en toda la gama de sus mutaciones y variantes, en los más empolvados museos de historia natural y en el corazón de todos los hombres.

Metamorphosis

Like a meteor that can flash out at noon with its own light, like a jewel that abruptly contradicts all the flies of the earth that fall into a plate of soup, the butterfly came in at the window and was shipwrecked immediately in the lentil broth.

Dazzled by its sudden brilliance (afterwards dispersed in the greasy surface of the greasy meal), the man gave up his routine feeding and set to work at once to salvage the prodigy. With the patience of one obsessed he picked out one by one the scales of that infinitesimal roof, he reconstructed from memory the design of the upper and lower wings, restoring to the antennae and the tiny feet their original grace, emptying and refilling the abdomen until he had attained the wasp waist that separates it from the thorax, carefully eliminating from each precious particle the least trace of fat, mess, and moisture.

The soup and the conjugal life cooled off once and for all. At the end of his labor, which consumed the best years of his life, the man realized with anguish that he had performed this taxidermy on a specimen of a common run-of-the-mill butterfly, an *Aphrodita vulgaris maculata*—a species that is found by the thousands, transfixed with pins, in the whole range of its mutations and variations, in the dustiest museums of natural history and in the heart of every man.

Translated by W. S. Merwin

ALI CHUMACERO
(nacido en Acaponeta, Nayarit 1918)

Uno de los fundadores de la revista *Tierra Nueva* (1940–42) y el suplemento cultural *Méjico en la Cultura*. Ha escrito numerosos artículos y ensayos de crítica literaria y ha preparado ediciones de las obras de otros poetas, como por ejemplo Xavier Villaurrutia y Alfonso Reyes. También es autor de algunos libros de poesía.

El orbe de la danza

Mueve los aires, torna en fuego
su propia mansedumbre: el frío
va al asombro y el resplandor
a música es llevado. Nadie
respira, nadie piensa y sólo
el ondear de las miradas
luce como una cabellera.
En la sala solloza el mármol
su orden recobrado, gime
el río de ceniza y cubre
rostros y trajes y humedad.
Cuerpo de acontecer o cima
en movimiento, su epitafio
impera en la penumbra y deja
desplomes, olas que no turban.
Muertas de oprobio, en el espacio
dormitan las familias, tristes
como el tahur aprisionado,
y añora la mujer adúltera
la caridad de ajena sábana.
Bajo la luz, la bailarina
sueña con desaparecer.

ALI CHUMACERO

(*born Acaponeta, Nayarit, 1918*)

One of the founders of the magazine *Tierra Nueva* (1940–42) and of the cultural supplement *Mexico en la Cultura*. He has written numerous articles and essays of literary criticism and has prepared editions of the works of other poets, Xavier Villaurrutia and Alfonso Reyes among others. He is the author of several books of poetry.

The Sphere of the Dance

She moves the air, her own gentleness
returns to fire: the cold
to amazement and the splendor
arises to music. No one
breathes, nobody thinks and only
the undulation of the glances
shimmers like hair a comet trails.
In the drawing room the marble sobs
its propriety recovered, the river
of ashes groans and hides
faces and clothes and humidity.
Body of happening or peak
in motion, its epitaph
prevails in the half-light and forsakes
collapsing, untumultuous waves.
Lifeless in ignominy, in space
the families doze, sad
as the imprisoned gambler,
and the adultress longs for
the charity of another's sheet.
Under the light, the dancer
dreams of disappearing.

Translated by Daniel Hoffman

EFRAÍN HUERTA
(*nacido en Silao, Guanajuato 1914*)

Periodista, que se especializa en crítica de cine, es también autor de
once libros de poesía, siendo el más reciente la colección completa de
sus poesías.

Los hombres del alba

Y después, aquí, en el oscuro seno del río más oscuro,
en lo más hondo y verde de la vieja ciudad,
estos hombres tatuados: ojos como diamantes,
bruscas bocas de odio más insomnio,
algunas rosas o azucenas en las manos
y una desesperante ráfaga de sudor.

Son los que tienen en vez de corazón
un perro enloquecido,
o una simple manzana luminosa,
o un frasco con saliva y alcohol,
o el murmullo de la una de la mañana,
o un corazón como cualquiera otro.

Son los hombres del alba.
Los bandidos con la barba crecida
y el bendito cinismo endurecido,
los asesinos cautelosos
con la ferocidad sobre los hombros,
los maricas con fiebre en las orejas
y en los blandos riñones,
los violadores,
los profesionales del desprecio,
los del aguardiente en las arterias,
los que gritan, aúllan, como lobos
con las patas heladas.
Los hombres más abandonados,
más locos, más valientes:
los más puros.

EFRAÍN HUERTA
(*born in Silao, Guanajuato, 1914*)

A journalist, specializing in movie criticism, he is the author of eleven
books of poetry, the most recent of which is his collected poems.

The Men of the Dawn

And after all, in the dark heart of the darkest river, here
in the green cellar of the old city,
these tattooed men, diamond eyed,
with mouths made crude by hatred and insomnia,
with roses or white lilies in their hands
and a desperate blast of sweat.

Those who have a mad dog
for a heart,
or a simple, luminous apple,
or a flask of alcohol and spit,
or a murmur of one o'clock in the morning,
or a heart like any other.

They are the men of the dawn.
Bandits with their beards grown full
and their blessed cynicism grown hard,
the careful assassins
with ferocity riding their shoulders,
cocksuckers with fevers in their ears
and their flabby kidneys,
the violators,
the professional scorners,
with booze in their arteries,
those who shout, howl, like wolves
with freezing paws.
Those who could care less,
the wildest, bravest:
the purest of men.

Ellos están caídos de sueño y esperanzas,
con los ojos en alto, la piel gris
y un eterno sollozo en la garganta.
Pero hablan. Al fin, la noche es una misma
siempre, y siempre fugitiva:
es un dulce tormento, un consuelo sencillo,
una negra sonrisa de alegría,
un modo diferente de conspirar,
una corriente tibia temerosa
de conocer la vida un poco envenenada.
Ellos hablan del día. Del día,
que no les pertenece, en que no se pertenecen,
en que son más esclavos; del día,
en que no hay más caminos
que un prolongado silencio
o una definitiva rebelión.

Pero yo sé que tienen miedo del alba.
Sé que aman la noche y sus lecciones escalofriantes.
Sé de la lluvia nocturna cayendo
como sobre cadáveres.
Sé que ellos construyen con sus huesos
un sereno monumento a la angustia.
Ellos y yo sabemos estas cosas:
que la gemidora metralla nocturna,
después de alborotar brazos y muertes,
después de oficiar apasionadamente
como madre del miedo,
se resuelve en rumor,
en penetrante ruido,
en cosa helada y acariciante,
en poderoso árbol con espinas plateadas,
en reseca alambrada:
en alba. En alba
con eficacia de pecho desafiante.

Entonces un dolor desnudo y terso
aparece en el mundo.
Y los hombres son pedazos de alba,
son tigres en guardia,
son pájaros entre hebras de plata,

They almost fall under the weight of sleep and all their hopes,
with their eyes raised, with their skin graying
and an endless sob in their throats.
But they talk. Finally, the night is always
the same, always fugitive:
a sweet torment, a simple consolation,
a black smile of joy,
another way of conspiring,
a lukewarm, hesitant way
of finding life slightly poisoned.
They speak of the day. The day
which isn't theirs and in which they don't belong,
in which they're slaves, the day
which has no roads
except a long silence
or a final rebellion.

I know they're afraid of the dawn.
I know they love the night and its chilling lessons.
I know the rain falling nightly,
falling as though on corpses.
I know they make out of their bones
a calm monument to anguish.
Together we know this:
that the wailing shellfire of night
after inciting the riot of arms and death,
and passionately officiating
as the mother of fear,
settles into rumor,
into piercing noises,
into something frozen and caressing,
into a powerful tree of silvered thorns,
into thirsting tangles of barbed wire:
into dawn. Into dawn
as skilled as a defiant chest.

Then a naked and polished sorrow
enters the world.
And men are pieces of the dawn,
tigers on their guard,
birds upon silver strings,

son escombros de voces.
Y el alba negrera se mete en todas partes:
en las raíces torturadas,
en las botellas estallantes de rabia,
en las orejas amoratadas,
en el húmedo desconsuelo de los asesinos,
en la boca de los niños dormidos.

Pero los hombres del alba se repiten
en forma clamorosa,
y ríen y mueren como guitarras pisoteadas,
con la cabeza limpia
y el corazón blindado.

La muchacha ebria

Este lánguido caer en brazos de una desconocida,
esta brutal tarea de pisotear mariposas y sombras y cadáveres;
este pensarse árbol, botella o chorro de alcohol,
huella de pie dormido, navaja verde o negra;
este instante durísimo en que una muchacha grita,
gesticula y sueña con una virtud que nunca fue la suya.
Todo esto no es sino la noche,
sino la noche grávida de sangre y leche,
de niños que se asfixian,
de mujeres carbonizadas
y varones morenos de soledad
y misterioso, sofocante desgaste.
Sino la noche de la muchacha ebria
cuyos gritos de rabia y melancolía
me hirieron como el llanto purísimo,
como las náuseas y el rencor,
como el abandono y la voz de las mendigas.
Lo triste es este llanto, amigos, hecho de vidrio molido
y fúnebres gardenias, despedazadas en el umbral de las cantinas,
llanto y sudor molidos, en que hombres desnudos, con sólo negra
    barba
y feas manos de miel se bañan sin angustia, sin tristeza;

the garbage of voices.
And the blackened dawn plunges everywhere:
into the tortured roots,
into bottles bursting with rage,
into bruised and beaten ears,
into the damp griefs of assassins,
into the mouths of sleeping children.

But the men of the dawn shout
as they always do
and they laugh and die like trampled guitars,
with a clean head
and an armored heart.

Translated by Philip Levine

The Drunken Girl

This crumpling into the arms of an unknown girl,
this brute job of trampling on butterflies, shadows, corpses;
this thinking of yourself as a tree, a bottle, or a flow of alcohol,
a print of a sleeping foot, a black or green jackknife;
this hard instant when a girl screams
and, shuddering, dreams of the goodness that was never hers.
All of this is not only the night,
but the night pregnant with blood and milk,
with asphyxiating children,
with women burned down to carbon
and men darkened by loneliness
and mysterious, suffocating waste.
Only the night of the drunken girl
whose sad, raging calls
wounded me like pure tears,
like nauseas and grudges,
like neglect and the begging of girls.
How sad these tears, friends, made of powdered glass
and funereal gardenias, shredded in the doorways of bars,
ground tears and sweat, in which naked men, with only black beards
and hands as ugly as honey wash themselves without anguish, with-
out sadness;

llanto ebrio, lágrimas de claveles, de tabernas enmohecidas,
de la muchacha que se embriaga sin tedio ni pesadumbre,
de la muchacha que una noche, y era una santa noche,
me entregara su corazón derretido,
sus manos de agua caliente, césped, seda,
sus pensamientos tan parecidos a pájaros muertos
sus torpes arrebatos de ternura,
su boca que sabía a taza mordida por dientes de borrachos,
su pecho suave como una mejilla con fiebre,
y sus brazos y piernas con tatuajes,
y su naciente tuberculosis,
y su dormido sexo de orquídea martirizada.
Ah la muchacha ebria, la muchacha del sonreír estúpido
y la generosidad en la punta de los dedos,
la muchacha de la confiada, inefable dulzura para un hombre,
como yo, escapado apenas de la violencia amorosa.
Este tierno recuerdo siempre será una lámpara frente a mis ojos,
una fecha sangrienta y abatida.

Por la muchacha ebria, amigos míos.

drunken crying, tears like carnations, like mildewed taverns,
tears like that girl's, neither bored nor grieving, who gets drunk,
like the girl's who one night, one holy night,
gave me her melting heart,
her hands of warm water, budding earth, silk,
her thoughts so like dead birds
her wooden seizures of tenderness,
her mouth tasting like a cup gnawed by drunks,
her breast soft as a fevered cheek,
her tattooed arms and legs,
her incipient tuberculosis,
and her cunt sleeping like a martyred orchid.
Ah, the drunken girl, the girl of the dumb smile
and generosity at her fingertips,
the girl of the trusting, unspeakable sweetness for a man,
a man like me, barely escaped from the violence of loving.
This tender memory will always be a lamp before my eyes,
a bloody and defeated day.

My friends, here's to the drunken girl.

Translated by Philip Levine

OCTAVIO PAZ
(nacido en Méjico D.F. 1914)

En el servicio exterior Mejicano desde 1945 hasta su renuncia en 1968 como embajador en la India. Ha publicado muchos libros de ensayos, muchas traducciones de poesía, obras de Matsúo Basto, Fernando Pessoa, ee cummings, George Schéhadé, Artur Lundkvist, entre otros—y más de una docena de volúmenes de su propia poesía.

Trabajos del poeta

I

A las tres y veinte como a las nueve y cuarenta y cuatro, desgreñados al alba y pálidos a medianoche, pero siempre puntualmente inesperados, sin trompetas, calzados de silencio, en general de negro, dientes feroces, voces roncas, todos ojos de bocaza, se presentan Tedevoro y Tevomito, Tli, Mundoinmundo, Carnaza, Carroña y Escarnio. Ninguno y los otros, que son mil y nadie, un minuto y jamás. Finjo no verlos y sigo mi trabajo, la conversación un instante suspendida, las sumas y las restas, la vida cotidiana. Secreta y activamente me ocupo de ellos. La nube preñada de palabras viene, dócil y sombría, a suspenderse sobre mi cabeza, balanceándose, mugiendo como un animal herido. Hundo la mano en ese saco caliginoso y extraigo lo que encuentro: un cuerno astillado, un rayo enmohecido, un hueso mondo. Con esos trastos me defiendo, apaleo a los visitantes, corto orejas, combato a brazo partido largas horas de silencio al raso. Crujir de dientes, huesos rotos, un miembro de menos, uno de más, en suma un juego—si logro tener los ojos bien abiertos y la cabeza fría—. Pero no hay que mostrar demasiada habilidad: una superioridad manifiesta los desanima. Y tampoco excesiva confianza; podrían aprovecharse, y entonces ¿quién responde de las consecuencias?

VII

Escribo sobre la mesa crepuscular, apoyando fuerte la pluma sobre su pecho casi vivo, que gime y recuerda al bosque natal. La tinta negra abre sus grandes alas. Pero la lámpara estalla y cubre mis palabras una capa de cristales rotos. Un fragmento afilado de luz me corta la mano derecha. Continúo escribiendo con ese muñón que mana sombra. La noche entra en el cuarto, el muro de enfrente adelanta su jeta de piedra, grandes témpanos de aire se interponen entre la pluma y el papel. Ah, un simple monosílabo bastaría para hacer saltar el mundo. Pero esta noche no hay sitio para una sola palabra más.

OCTAVIO PAZ
(born in Mexico, D.F., 1914)

In the Mexican foreign service from 1945 until his resignation as Ambassador to India in 1968, he has published many books of essays, many translations of poetry—works by Matsuo Basho, Fernando Pessoa, e e cummings, George Schehade, Artur Lundkvist, among others —and over a dozen volumes of his own poetry.

Works of the Poet

I

At three twenty as at nine forty-four, disheveled at dawn and pale at midnight, but always punctually unexpected, without trumpets, shod in silence, generally in black, with fierce teeth, hoarse voices, and large-mouthed eyes, Ichewyou and Ipukeyou, Tli, Dirtyworld, Fleshy, Carrionne and Mock present themselves. None and the others, that are one thousand and no one, a minute and never. I pretend not to see them and continue my work, the conversation an instant suspended, the additions and subtractions, the daily life. Secretly and actively, I am busy with them. Docile and shady, the pregnant cloud of words comes to hang over my head, wavering, roaring like a wounded animal. I put my hand into the dark bag and pull out what I find: a chipped horn, a rusty spoke, a clean bone. With this trash I defend myself, beating up the visitors, cutting ears, fighting hand to hand for long hours of silence in the open air. Gnash of teeth, broken bones, a limb less, one more, in sum a game—if I am to succeed having my eyes open and my head clear. But there is no need to show too much cunning: a manifest superiority dispirits them. And likewise excessive confidence: they can avail themselves, and then, who answers to the consequences?

VII

I write on the crepuscular table, heavily resting my pen on its chest that is almost living, that screams and remembers the forest of its birth. The black ink opens its great wings. The lamp explodes and covers my words with a cape of broken glass. A sharp sliver of light cuts off my right hand. I continue writing with that stump sprung from shadow. The night enters the room, the opposite wall puckers its fat stone lips, great drums of air pass between my pen and the paper. Oh, a simple monosyllable would be enough to make the world leap! But tonight there is no room for another syllable more.

XIII

Hace años, con piedrecitas, basuras y yerbas, edifiqué Tilantlán. Recuerdo la muralla, las puertas amarillas con el signo digital, las calles estrechas y malolientes que habitaba una plebe ruidosa, el verde Palacio del Gobierno y la roja Casa de los Sacrificios, abierta como una mano, con sus cinco grandes templos y sus calzadas innumerables. Tilantlán, ciudad gris al pie de la piedra blanca, ciudad agarrada al suelo con uñas y dientes, ciudad de polvo y plegarias. Sus moradores —astutos, ceremoniosos y coléricos—adoraban a las Manos, que los habían hecho, pero temían a los Pies, que podrían destruirlos. Su teología, y los renovados sacrificios con que intentaron comprar el amor de las Primeras y asegurarse la benevolencia de los Últimos, no evitaron que una alegre mañana mi pie derecho los aplastara, con su historia, su aristocracia feroz, sus motines, su lenguaje sagrado, sus canciones populares y su teatro ritual. Y sus sacerdotes jamás sospecharon que Pies y Manos no eran sino las extremidades de un mismo dios.

XV

¡Pueblo mío, pueblo que mis magros pensamientos alimentan con migajas, con exhaustas imágenes penosamente extraídas de la piedra! Hace siglos que no llueve. Hasta la yerba rala de mi pecho ha sido secada por el sol. El cielo, limpio de estrellas y de nubes, está cada día más alto. Mi sangre se extenúa entre venas endurecidas. Nada te aplaca ya, Cólera, centella que te rompes los dientes contra el Muro; nada a vosotras, Virgen, Estrella Airada, hermosuras con alas, hermosuras con garras. Todas las palabras han muerto de sed. Nadie podrá alimentarse con estos restos pulidos, ni siquiera mis perros, mis vicios. Esperanza, águila famélica, déjame sobre esta roca parecida al silencio. Y tú, viento que soplas del Pasado, sopla con fuerza, dispersa estas pocas sílabas y hazlas aire y transparencia. ¡Ser al fin una Palabra, un poco de aire en una boca pura, un poco de agua en unos labios ávidos! Pero ya el olvido pronuncia mi nombre: míralo brillar entre sus labios como el hueco que brilla un instante en el hocico de la noche de negro pelaje. Los cantos que no dije, los cantos del arenal, los dice el viento de una sola vez, en una sola frase interminable, sin principio, sin fin y sin sentido.

XIII

Years ago, with pebbles, garbage and grass, I built Tilantlan. I remember the walls, the yellow doors with the digital sign, the long and diarrheal streets that sheltered a noisy populace, the green Governor's Palace and the red House of the Sacrifices, open like a hand, with its five great temples and its countless causeways. Tilantlan, gray city at the foot of the white rock, city brought to the floor with nails and teeth; city of dust and prayers. Its inhabitants—astute, ceremonious, and passionate—worshipped the Hands that had made them, but feared the Feet that could destroy them. Their theology, and the fresh sacrifices with which they intended to buy the love of the Firsts and insure the benevolence of the Lasts did not spare them that happy morning when my right foot crushed them and their history, their fierce aristocracy, their insurrections, their sacred language, their folk songs and ritual theater. Their priests never suspected that Feet and Hands were nothing but extremities of the same god.

XV

My people, people whom my lean thoughts fed with scraps, with tired images painfully pulled from stone! For centuries it has not rained. Until even the sparse grass on my chest has been shriveled by the sun. The sky, clear of stars and clouds, each day is higher. My blood moves through hardened veins. No one appeases you, Anger, flashing as you break your teeth against the Wall; nothing for you two, Virgin and Wrathful Star, you beauties with wings, beauties with claws. All of the words have died from thirst. No one will feed themselves with these polished remains, not even my dogs, my vices. Hope, emaciated eagle, leave me on this rock like silence. And you, wind that blows from the Past, blow fiercely, scatter these few syllables and make them air and transparency. To be finally a Word, a bit of air in a pure mouth, a bit of water on greedy lips! But now the forgetfulness pronounces my name: watch it shine between his lips like a bone that shines a moment in the snout of the night of black hair. The cantos that I never said, the cantos of sand, are said by the wind a single time in a single interminable phrase, sourceless, endless, senseless.

Translated by Eliot Weinberger

Madrugada

Rápidas manos frías
Retiran una a una
Las vendas de la sombra
Abro los ojos
        Todavía
Estoy vivo
      En el centro
De una herida todavía fresca.

Aquí

Mis pasos en esta calle
Resuenan
      En otra calle
Donde
     Oigo mis pasos
Pasar en esta calle
Donde

Sólo es real la niebla.

Viento entero

a Marie José

El presente es perpetuo
Los montes son de hueso y son de nieve
Están aquí desde el principio
El viento acaba de nacer
          Sin edad
Como la luz y como el polvo

Dawn

Quick cold hands
One by one remove
The bandages from the darkness
I open my eyes
                    I am alive
Still
    In the middle
Of a wound still fresh.

Translated by Eliot Weinberger

Here

My footsteps on this street
Resound
            In another street
Where
        I hear my footsteps
Stepping on this street
Where

Only the mist is real.

Translated by Eliot Weinberger

Wind from All Compass Points

To Marie José

The present is motionless
The mountains are of bone and of snow
They have been here since the beginning
The wind has just been born
                        Ageless
As the light and the dust

Molino de sonidos
El bazar tornasolea
Timbres motores radios
El trote pétreo de los asnos opacos
Cantos y quejas enredados
Entre las barbas de los comerciantes
Alto fulgor a martillazos esculpido
En los claros de silencio
Estallan
Los gritos de los niños
Príncipes en harapos
A la orilla del río atormentado
Rezan orinan meditan
El presente es perpetuo
Se abren las compuertas del año
El día salta
Ágata
El pájaro caído
Entre la calle Montalambert y la de Bac
Es una muchacha
Detenida
Sobre un precipicio de miradas
Si el agua es fuego
Llama
En el centro de la hora redonda
Encandilada
Potranca alazana
Un haz de chispas
Una muchacha real
Entre las casas y las gentes espectrales
Presencia chorro de evidencias
Yo vi a través de mis actos irreales
La tomé de la mano
Juntos atravesamos
Los cuatro espacios los tres tiempos
Pueblos errantes de reflejos
Y volvimos al día del comienzo
El presente es perpetuo
21 de junio
Hoy comienza el verano
Dos o tres pájaros

                    A windmill of sounds
The bazaar spins its colors
                    Bells motors radios
The stony trot of dark donkeys
Songs and complaints entangled
Among the beards of the merchants
The tall light chiseled with hammer strokes
In the clearings of silence
                    Boys' cries
        Explode
Princes in tattered clothes
On the banks of the tortured river
Pray pee meditate
                    The present is motionless
The floodgates of the year open
                    Day flashes out
        Agate
    The fallen bird
Between rue Montalambert and rue de Bac
Is a girl
            Held back
At the edge of a precipice of looks
If water is fire
                Flame
                Dazzled
In the center of the spherical hour
            A sorrel filly
A marching batallion of sparks
                        A real girl
Among wraithlike houses and people
Presence a fountain of reality
I looked out through my own unrealities
I took her hand
                Together we crossed
The four quadrants the three times
Floating tribes of reflections
And we returned to the day of beginning
The present is motionless
                    June 21st
Today is the beginning of summer
                    Two or three birds

Inventan un jardín
                    Tú lees y comes un durazno
Sobre la colcha roja
                    Desnuda
Como el vino en el cántaro de vidrio
                    Un gran vuelo de cuervos
En Santo Domingo mueren nuestros hermanos
Si hubiera parque no estarían ustedes aquí
                    Nosotros nos roemos los codos
En los jardines de su alcázar de estío
Tipú Sultán plantó el árbol de los jacobinos
Luego distribuyó pedazos de vidrio
Entre los oficiales ingleses prisioneros
Y ordenó que se cortasen el prepucio
Y se lo comiesen
                    El siglo
Se ha encendido en nuestras tierras
Con su lumbre
                    Las manos abrasadas
Los constructores de catedrales y pirámides
Levantarán sus casas transparentes
                              El presente es perpetuo
El sol se ha dormido entre tus pechos
La colcha roja es negra y palpita
Ni astro ni alhaja
                    Fruta
Túte llamas dátil
                    Datia
Castillo de sal si puedes
                              Mancha escarlata
Sobre la piedra empedernida
Galerías terrazas escaleras
Desmanteladas salas nupciales
Del escorpión
                    Ecos repeticiones
Relojería erótica
                    Deshora
                    Tú recorres
Los patios taciturnos bajo la tarde impía
Manto de agujas en tus hombros indemnes
Si el fuego es agua

Invent a garden
        You read and eat a peach
On the red couch
        Naked
Like the wine in the glass pitcher
        A great flock of crows
Our brothers are dying in Santo Domingo
If we had the munitions you people would not be here
        We chew our nails down to the elbow
In the gardens of his summer fortress
Tipoo Sultan planted the Jacobin tree
Then distributed glass shards among
The imprisoned English officials
And ordered them to cut their foreskins
And eat them
        The century
Has caught fire in our lands
From that blaze
        With scorched hands
The cathedral and pyramid builders
Will raise their transparent houses
        The present is motionless
The sun has fallen asleep between your breasts
The red covering is black and heaves
Not planet and not jewel
        Fruit
You are named Date
        Datia
Castle of Leave-If-You-Can
        Scarlet stain
Upon the obdurate stone
Corridors terraces stairways
Dismantled nuptial chambers
Of the scorpion
        Echoes   repetitions
The intricate and erotic works of a watch
        Beyond time
        You cross
Taciturn patios under the pitiless afternoon
A cloak of needles on your untouched shoulders
If fire is water

Eres una gota diáfana
La muchacha real
Transparencia del mundo
El presente es perpetuo
Los montes
Soles destazados
Petrificada tempestad ocre
El viento rasga
Ver duele
El cielo es otro abismo más alto
Garganta de Salang
La nube negra sobre la roca negra
El puño de la sangre golpea
Puertas de piedra
Sólo el agua es humana
En estas soledades despeñadas
Sólo tus ojos de agua humana
Abajo
En el espacio hendido
El deseo te cubre con sus dos alas negras
Tus ojos se abren y se cierran
Animales fosforescentes
Abajo
El desfiladero caliente
La ola que se dilata y se rompe
Tus piernas abiertas
El salto blanco
La espuma de nuestros cuerpos abandonados
El presente es perpetuo
El morabito regaba la tumba del santo
Sus barbas eran más blancas que las nubes
Frente al moral
Al flanco del torrente
Repetiste mi nombre
Dispersión de sílabas
Un adolescente de ojos verdes te regaló
Una granada
Al otro lado del Amu-Darya
Humeaban las casitas rusas
El son de la flauta usbek
Era otro río invisible y más puro

                    You are a diaphanous drop
The real girl
                    Transparency of the world
The present is motionless
                              The mountains
                       Quartered suns
Petrified storm earth-yellow
                              The wind whips
                                        It hurts to see
The sky is another deeper abyss
Gorge of the Salang Pass
Black cloud over black rock
Fist of blood strikes
                       Gates of stone
Only the water is human
In these precipitous solitudes
Only your eyes of human water
                              Down there
In the cleft place
Desire covers you with its two black wings
Your eyes flash open and close
                              Phosphorescent animals
Down there
              The hot canyon
The wave that stretches and breaks
                       Your legs apart
The plunging whiteness
The foam of our bodies abandoned
                              The present is motionless
The hermit watered the saint's tomb
His beard was whiter than the clouds
Facing the mulberry
                    On the flank of the rushing stream
You repeat my name
                    Dispersion of syllables
A young man with green eyes presented you
With a pomegranate
                    On the other bank of the Amu-Darya
Smoke rose from Russian cottages
The sound of an Usbek flute
Was another river   invisible   clearer

En la barcaza el batelero estrangulaba pollos
El país es una mano abierta
Sus líneas
Signos de un alfabeto roto
Osamentas de vacas en el llano
Bactriana
Estatua pulverizada
Yo recogí del polvo unos cuantos nombres
Por esas sílabas caídas
Granos de una granada cenicienta
Juro ser tierra y viento
Remolino
Sobre tus huesos
El presente es perpetuo
La noche entra con todos sus árboles
Noche de insectos eléctricos y fieras de seda
Noche de yerbas que andan sobre los muertos
Conjunción de aguas que vienen de lejos
Murmullos
Los universos se desgranan
Un mundo cae
Se enciende una semilla
Cada palabra palpita
Oigo tu latir en la sombra
Enigma en forma de reloj de arena
Mujer dormida
Espacio espacios animados
Anima mundi
Materia maternal
Perpetua desterrada de sí misma
Y caída perpetua en su entraña vacía
Anima mundi
Madre de las razas errantes
De soles y de hombres
Emigran los espacios
El presente es perpetuo
En el pico del mundo se acarician
Shiva y Parvati
Cada caricia dura un siglo
Para el dios y para el hombre
Un mismo tiempo

The boatman
              On the barge was strangling chickens
The countryside is an open hand
                          Its lines
              Marks of a broken alphabet
Cow skeletons on the prairie
Bactria
          A shattered statue
I scraped a few names out of the dust
By these fallen syllables
Seeds of a charred pomegranate
I swear to be earth and wind
                          Whirling
Over your bones
                  The present is motionless
Night comes down with its trees
Night of electric insects and silken beasts
Night of grasses which cover the dead
Meetings of waters which come from far off
Rustlings
              Universes are strewn about
A world falls
                  A seed flares up
Each word beats
                      I hear you throb in the shadow
A riddle shaped like an hourglass
                              Woman asleep
Space   living spaces
Anima mundi
                  Maternal substance
Always torn from itself
Always falling into your empty womb
                              Anima mundi
Mother of the nomadic tribes
                          Of suns and men
The spaces turn
                              The present is motionless
At the top of the world
Shiva and Parvati caress
                      Each caress lasts a century
For the god and for the man
                          An identical time

Un mismo despeñarse
                    Lahor
                        Río rojo barcas negras
Entre dos tamarindos una niña descalza
Y su mirar sin tiempo
                    Un latido idéntico
Muerte y nacimiento
Entre el cielo y la tierra suspendidos
Unos cuantos álamos
Vibrar de luz más que vaivén de hojas
                                ¿Suben o bajan?
El presente es perpetuo
                    Llueve sobre mi infancia
Llueve sobre el jardín de la fiebre
Flores de sílex árboles de humo
En una hoja de higuera tú navegas
Por mi frente
                La lluvia no te moja
Eres la llama de agua
                    La gota diáfana de fuego
Derramada sobre mis párpados
Yo veo a través de mis actos irreales
El mismo día que comienza
                        Gira el espacio
Arranca sus raíces el mundo
No pesan más que el alba nuestros cuerpos
                                Tendidos

An equivalent hurling headlong
                              Lahore
                    Red river   black boats
A barefoot girl between two tamarinds
And her timeless gaze
                    An identical throbbing
Death and birth
A group of poplars
Suspended between sky and earth
They are a quiver of light more than a trembling of leaves
                    Do they rise or fall?
The present is motionless
                              It rains on my childhood
It rains on the feverish garden
Flint flowers   trees of smoke
In a figleaf you sail on my brow
                    The rain does not wet you
You are flame of water
                    The diaphanous drop of fire
Spilling upon my eyelids
I look out through my own unrealities
The same day is beginning
                              Space wheels
The world wrenches up its roots
Our bodies
              Stretched out
                    Weigh no more than dawn

Translated by Paul Blackburn

GILBERTO OWEN

(*nacido en El Rosario, Sinaloa, 1905; fallecido en Philadelphia, 1952*)

Miembro de la generación de "contemporaneos," publicó cuatro libros: *Linea* (1930), *El Libro de Ruth* (1944), *Perseo Vencido* (1948), and *Poesía y Prosa* (1953).

Interior

Las cosas que entran por el silencio empiezan a llegar al cuarto. Lo sabemos, porque nos dejamos olvidados allá adentro los ojos. La soledad llega por los espejos vacíos; la muerte baja de los cuadros, rompiendo sus vitrinas de museo; los rincones se abren como granadas para que entre el grillo con sus alfileres; y, aunque nos olvidemos de apagar la luz, la oscuridad da una luz negra más potente que eclipsa a la otra.

Pero no son éstas las cosas que entran por el silencio, sino otras más sutiles aún; si nos hubiéramos dejado olvidada también la boca, sabríamos nombrarlas. Para sugerirlas, los preceptistas aconsejan hablar de paralelas que, sin dejar de serlo, se encuentran y se besan. Pero los niños que resuelven ecuaciones de segundo grado se suicidan siempre en cuanto llegan a los ochenta años, y preferimos por eso mirar sin nombres lo que entra por el silencio, y dejar que todos sigan afirmando que dos y dos son cuatro.

GILBERTO OWEN

(*born in El Rosario, Sinaloa, 1905; died in Philadelphia, 1952*)

A member of the generation of "*contemporaneos*," he published four books: *Linea* (1930), *El Libro de Ruth* (1944), *Perseo Vencido* (1948), and *Poesía y Prosa* (1953).

Interior

Things that enter by way of silence are beginning to come into the room. We know because we left our eyes there. Solitude comes in through the empty mirrors; death steps down from the pictures, breaking the museum casings; the corners open like pomegranates so the cricket and its feelers might enter; and, though we forgot to put out the light, the darkness gives off a stronger black light that eclipses it.

But these are not the things that enter by way of silence, there are other things yet more subtle. If we had also left our mouths behind, we would have known what to call them. To inspire them counselors advise speaking of parallels that meet each other and kiss without ceasing to be what they are. But children who solve quadratic equations commit suicide as soon as they get to be eighty years old, and that's why we'd rather look at whatever comes in with the silence without naming it, and let everyone keep on claiming that two and two make four.

Translated by Mark Strand

SALVADOR NOVO
(*nacido en Méjico D.F. 1904*)

Conjunto con Xavier Villaurrutia fundó la revista *Ulises* (1927–28).
Muy conocido por sus antologías y ensayos, es autor de ocho libros de
poesía, el más reciente es la edición de 1961 de todos sus poemas, reu-
nidos bajo el titulo *Poesía*.

Del pasado remoto
[*Fragmento*]

Del pasado remoto
sobre las grandes pirámides de Teotihuacán,
sobre los teocalis y los volcanes,
sobre los huesos y las cruces de los conquistadores áureos
crece el tiempo en silencio.

Hojas de hierba
en el polvo, en las tumbas frías;
Whitman amaba su perfume inocente y salvaje
y Sandburg lo ha visto cubrir las tumbas
de Napoleón y de Lincoln.

Nuestros héroes
han sido vestidos como marionetas
y machacados en las hojas de los libros
para veneración y recuerdo de la niñez estudiosa,
y el Padre Hildalgo,
Morelos y la Corregidora de Querétaro,
con sus peinetas y su papada, de perfil siempre,
y Morelos con su levita, sus botas negras y su trapo
en la cabeza, feroz el gesto, caudillo suriano
y la Corte de los virreyes de terciopelo, hierro y encajes
y la figura de cera de Xóchil descalza
entre los magueyes de cera verde.

Luego Iturbide en su coronación
—¡y pudiste prestar fácil oído a falaz ambición!—
y nuevas causas de la libertad,
intervenciones de *cowboys* y zuavos de circo
y "entre renuevos cuyos aliños
un viento nuevo marchita en flor,
los héroes niños cierran sus alas

SALVADOR NOVO
(born in Mexico, D.F., 1904)

With Xavier Villaurrutia he founded the magazine *Ulises* (1927–28).
Well known as an anthologist and essayist, he is the author of eight
books of poetry, the most recent being the 1961 edition of his col-
lected poems, *Poesía*.

From the Remote Past (A Fragment)

From the remote past
over the great pyramids of Teotihuacan,
over the teocallis and volcanoes,
over the bones and crosses of the golden conquerors
time quietly grows.

Leaves of grass
in the dust, in the cold tombs;
Whitman loved their innocent and wild perfume
and Sandburg has seen them cover the tombs
of Napoleon and of Lincoln.

Our heroes
have been dressed like puppets
and crushed in the leaves of books
in honor and memory of studious childhoods,
and Father Hidalgo,
Morelos and the wife of the Mayor of Querétaro,
with her ornamental combs and her double chin, always in profile,
and Morelos with his frock coat, black boots and the bandanna
tied around his head, fierce-looking, surian leader
and the Court of the viceroys of velvet, iron and lace
and the wax figures of Xóchil barefoot
among the magueys of green wax.

Then Iturbide during his coronation
". . . and you lent an easy ear to deceitful ambition . . ."
and new causes of freedom,
interruptions of gringo *cowboys* and frog legionnaires
and "among boughs whose blossoms
a new wind withers
the child heroes fold their wings

bajo las balas del invasor".
Y Juárez, Benemérito de las Américas,
para que vean de lo que son capaces los indios,
en su litografía de marco dorado
sobre todos los pupitres grises, decorado de moscas,
sobre los pizarrones encanecidos,
el Monte de las Cruces, el Cerro de las Campanas,
el Cerro de Guadalupe
y don Porfirio y las fiestas del Centenario
a que vino Polavieja, entre otros,
y las *extras* de los periódicos
y el temblor de tierra que trajo a Madero
y a la señora Sara P. de Madero.

REVOLUCIÓN, REVOLUCIÓN,
siguen los héroes vestidos de marionetas,
vestidos con palabras signaléticas,
el usurpador Huerta
y la Revolución triunfante,
don Venustiano disfrazado con barbas y anteojos
como en una novela policíaca primitiva
y la Revolución Constitucionalista,
Obregón, que tiró la piedra y escondió la mano
y la Revolución triunfante de nuevo,
la Era de las Instituciones,
el Mensaje a la Nación,
las enseñanzas agrarias del nuevo caudillo suriano,
el Jefe Máximo de la Revolución,
y el Instituto Político de la Revolución,
los Postulados de la Revolución,
los intereses colectivos.
la clase laborante y el proletariado organizado,
la ideología clasista,
los intelectuales revolucionarios,
los pensadores al servicio del proletariado,
el campesinaje mexicano,
la Villa Álvaro Obregón, con su monumento,
y el Monumento a la Revolución.

La literatura de la Revolución
la poesía revolucionaria

under the bullets of the invader."
And Juarez, Meritorious of the Americas,
proof of what an Indian can do,
in his gold-framed lithograph
over all the gray desks, decorated by flies,
over the moldy blackboards,
the Mount of the Crosses, the Hill of the Bells,
the Peak of Guadalupe
and don Porfirio and the celebrations of the Centennial
to which came Polavieja, among others,
and the *extras* of the newspapers
and the earthquake which brought Madero
and Mrs. Sara P. de Madero.

REVOLUTION, REVOLUTION,
the heroes dressed like puppets go on,
adorned with signaletic words,
the usurper Huerta
and the triumphant Revolution,
don Venustiano masquerading with beard and glasses
as in early detective novels
and the Constitutionalist Revolution,
Obregón, who threw the stone and hid his hand
and the triumphant Revolution again,
the Age of the Institutions,
the Message to the Nation,
the agrarian teachings of the new surian leader,
the Highest Leader of the Revolution,
and the Political Institute of the Revolution,
the Postulates of the Revolution,
the collective interests,
the laboring class and the organized proletariat,
the classicist ideology,
the revolutionary intellectuals,
the intellectuals at the service of the proletariat,
the Mexican peasantry,
the Villa Alvaro Obregón, with its monument,
and the Monument of the Revolution.

The literature of the Revolution
the revolutionary poetry

alrededor de tres o cuatro anécdotas de Villa
y el florecimiento de los máussers,
las rúbricas del lazo, la soldadera,
las cartucheras y las mazorcas,
la hoz y el Sol, hermano pintor proletario,
los corridos y las canciones del campesino
y el overol azul del cielo,
la sirena estrangulada de la fábrica
y el ritmo nuevo de los martillos
de los hermanos obreros
y los parches verdes de los ejidos
de que los hermanos campesinos
han echado al espantapájaros del cura

Los folletos de propaganda revolucionaria,
el Gobierno al servicio del proletariado,
los intelectuales proletarios al servicio del Gobierno,
los radios al servicio de los intelectuales proletarios
al servicio del Gobierno de la Revolución
para repetir incesantemente sus postulados
hasta que se graben en las mentes de los proletarios
—de los proletarios que tengan radio y los escuchen.

Crece el tiempo en silencio,
hojas de hierba, polvo de las tumbas
que agita apenas la palabra.

Roberto, el subteniente

Cuando salió del Colegio y cumplió veintiún años
y ostentó en la gorra la barra de subteniente,
llegó al cuartel con una gran energía acumulada.
En el Colegio todo era perfecto y limpio,
la gimnasia y la equitación lo habían hecho fuerte y ligero
y conocía perfectamente la historia antigua
y todas las campañas de Napoleón.
Iba a ganar ya sueldo.
Cuatro pesos son mucho dinero para uno solo.

around three or four anecdotes of Villa
and the flourishing of rifles,
the looping signatures of the lasso, the camp followers,
the cartridge boxes and the corncobs,
the sickle and the Sun, proletarian brother painter,
the "corridos" * and the folk songs
and the dungaree blue of the sky,
the stifled siren of the factory
and the new rhythm of the hammers
of the brother workers
and the green patches of communal lands
from which the brother peasants
have thrown off the scarecrow of the priest.

The pamphlets of revolutionary propaganda,
the government at the service of the Proletariat,
the intellectual proletarians at the service of the Government,
the radios at the service of the proletarian intellectuals
at the service of the Government of the Revolution
to incessantly repeat its postulates
until they are recorded in the minds of the proletariat
—of the proletariat who would have radios and would listen to them.

Time quietly grows,
leaves of grass, dust of the tombs
scarcely shaken by the word.   *Translated by Suzanne Jill Levine*

* Mexican folk song and dance.

Roberto, the Second Lieutenant

When he left the Academy and turned twenty-one
and displayed on his cap his second lieutenant's bar,
he arrived at the barracks with lots of stored-up energy.
At the Academy everything was perfect and clean,
gymnastics and riding had made him strong and agile
and he knew ancient history perfectly
and all the campaigns of Napoleon.
He was all set to earn a living.
Four pesos is a lot of money for one person.

Le dieron un asistente que le traía la comida
y le quitaba las botas, o le ensillaba el caballo.
A diana, se levantaba
e iba a dar instrucción a los soldados
y luego hacía guardia en la puerta
toda la mañana muerta y ociosa,
toda una tarde llena de moscas y de polvo
hasta que llamaban a lista de seis
y asistía a la complicada ceremonia
de la lectura de la Orden del Día.
Entonces, con la sombra,
despertaban sus más primitivos instintos
y reunido con otros oficiales
bebía tequila hasta embriagarse
e iba a buscar a una mujerzuela
para golpearla despiadadamente
azotándola como a su caballo,
mordiéndola hasta la sangre,
insultándola hasta hacerla llorar
y luego acariciándola con ternura,
dándole todo su cuerpo febril y joven,
para marcharse luego al cuartel
abriéndose paso, a puntapiés, hasta su habitación,
entre los soldados que yacían en la sombra, sin almohada,
enlazados a sus mujeres o a sus fusiles.

They gave him a helper who brought him his meals
and took off his boots, or saddled his horse.
At reveille, he got up
and went out to give orders to the soldiers
and then stood guard at the door
the whole dead and wasting morning,
the whole afternoon full of flies and dust
until six o'clock roll call
and he attended the complicated ceremony
of the reading of The Order of The Day.
Then, with the dark,
his most primitive instincts awoke
and he joined the other officers
drank tequila until drunk
and went to look for a little woman
to beat her unmercifully
whipping her like a horse,
biting her until she bled,
insulting her until he made her cry
and then tenderly embracing her,
giving her all of his feverish, young body,
to go then to the barracks
making his way, kicking, to his room
among the soldiers who lay in the dark, without pillows,
bound up with their women or their guns.

Translated by Suzanne Jill Levine

XAVIER VILLAURRUTIA

(*nacido en Méjico D.F. 1903, fallecido en Méjico D.F. 1950*)

Con Salvador Novo fundó la revista *Ulises* (1927–28) más tarde se asoció con la revista *Contemporáneos* (1928–31) y *El Hijo Pródigo* (1943–46). También es el autor de muchos libros de poesía.

Nocturno de la estatua

a Agustín Lazo

Soñar, soñar la noche, la calle, la escalera
y el grito de la estatua desdoblando la esquina.
Correr hacia la estatua y encontrar sólo el grito,
querer tocar el grito y sólo hallar el eco,
querer asir el eco y encontrar sólo el muro
y correr hacia el muro y tocar un espejo.
Hallar en el espejo la estatua asesinada,
sacarla de la sangre de su sombra,
vestirla en un cerrar de ojos,
acariciarla como a una hermana imprevista
y jugar con las fichas de sus dedos
y contar a su oreja cien veces cien cien veces
hasta oírla decir: "estoy muerta de sueño".

Nocturno eterno

Cuando los hombres alzan los hombros y pasan
o cuando dejan caer sus nombres
hasta que la sombra se asombra

cuando un polvo más fino aún que el humo
se adhiere a los cristales de la voz
y a la piel de los rostros y las cosas

cuando los ojos cierran sus ventanas
el rayo del sol pródigo y prefieren
la ceguera al perdón y el silencio al sollozo

XAVIER VILLAURRUTIA

(born in Mexico, D.F., 1903; died in Mexico, D.F., 1950)

With Salvador Novo he founded the magazine *Ulises* (1927–28), later became connected with the magazine *Contemporáneos* (1928–31) and *El Hijo Prodigo* (1943–46). He is the author of many books of poetry.

Nocturne of the Statue

to Agustín Lazo

To dream, to dream the night, the street, the stair
and the cry of the statue turning back at the corner.
To run toward the statue and to meet the cry only,
to want to touch the cry and only find the echo,
to want to seize the echo and to meet the wall only,
and to run toward the wall and touch a mirror.
To find the statue murdered in the mirror,
to draw it forth from the blood of its shadow,
to dress it, closing the eyes,
to caress it like a sister not foreseen,
and to ply the ends of its fingers,
and to count in its ear a hundred times a hundred hundred times
until one hears it say: "I am dead tired."

Translated by Donald Justice

Eternal Nocturne

When men raise their shoulders and pass on
or when they let their names fall
until the shadow is darkened

when a dust even finer than smoke
adheres to the windows of the voice
and the skin of cheeks and things

when eyes close their windows
to the rays of the prodigal sun and prefer
blindness to absolution and silence to sobbing

cuando la vida o lo que así llamamos inútilmente
y que no llega sino con un nombre innombrable
se desnuda para saltar al lecho
y ahogarse en el alcohol o quemarse en la nieve

cuando la vi cuando la vid cuando la vida
quiere entregarse cobardemente y a oscuras
sin decirnos siquiera el precio de su nombre

cuando en la soledad de un cielo muerto
brillan unas estrellas olvidadas
y es tan grande el silencio del silencio
que de pronto quisiéramos que hablara

o cuando de una boca que no existe
sale un grito inaudito
que nos echa a la cara su luz viva
y se apaga y nos deja una ciega sordera

o cuando todo ha muerto
tan dura y lentamente que da miedo
alzar la voz y preguntar "quién vive"
dudo si responder
a la muda pregunta con un grito
por temor de saber que ya no existo

porque acaso la voz tampoco vive
sino como un recuerdo en la garganta
y no es la noche sino la ceguera
lo que llena de sombra nuestros ojos

y porque acaso el grito es la presencia
de una palabra antigua
opaca y muda que de pronto grita

porque vida silencio piel y boca
y soledad recuerdo cielo y humo
nada son sino sombras de palabras
que nos salen al paso de la noche.

when life or what we futilely call life
and which only comes with an unnamable name
undresses to jump into bed
and drown itself in alcohol or burn in snow

when I when lie when life
wants to surrender in cowardice and darkness
without even telling us the price of its name

when in the loneliness of a dead sky
forgotten stars gleam
and the silence's silence is so great
that we suddenly want it to speak

or when from a nonexistent mouth
there issues an inaudible cry
that hurls its glaring light in our faces
and dies away leaving us in blind deafness

or when everything has died
so terribly and so slowly that we are afraid
to raise our voices and ask "who's alive"
I hesitate to answer
the mute question with a cry
for fear of learning that I no longer exist

because perhaps our voices are not alive either
but are like memories in our throats
and it is not night but blindness
that fills our eyes with shadow

and because perhaps the cry is the presence
of an ancient word
opaque and mute crying out suddenly

because life silence skin and mouth
and solitude memory sky and smoke
are nothing but shadows of words
that issue from us at the night's passing.

Translated by Rachel Benson

Nocturna rosa

a José Gorostiza

Yo también hablo de la rosa.
Pero mi rosa no es la rosa fría
ni la de piel de niño,
ni la rosa que gira
tan lentamente que su movimiento
es una misteriosa forma de la quietud.

No es la rosa sedienta,
ni la sangrante llaga,
ni la rosa coronada de espinas,
ni la rosa de la resurrección.

No es la rosa de pétalos desnudos,
ni la rosa encerada,
ni la llama de seda,
ni tampoco la rosa llamarada.

No es la rosa veleta,
ni la úlcera secreta,
ni la rosa puntual que da la hora,
ni la brújula rosa marinera.

No, no es la rosa rosa
sino la rosa increada,
la sumergida rosa,
la nocturna,
la rosa inmaterial,
la rosa hueca.
Es la rosa del tacto en las tinieblas,
es la rosa que avanza enardecida,
la rosa de rosadas uñas,
la rosa yema de los dedos ávidos,
la rosa digital
la rosa ciega.

Es la rosa moldura del oído,
la rosa oreja,

Rose Nocturnal

to José Gorostiza

I too speak of the rose.
But my rose is neither the cold rose
nor the one in a child's skin,
nor the rose which turns
so slowly that its motion
is a mysterious form of stillness.

It is not the thirsty rose,
nor the wound bleeding,
nor the rose crowned with thorns,
nor the rose of the resurrection.

It is not the rose with naked petals,
nor the wax rose,
nor the silken flame,
nor yet the quick-blushing rose.

It is not the banner rose,
nor the secret garden-rot,
nor the punctual rose telling the hour,
nor the compass rose of the mariner.

No, it is not the rose rose
but the uncreated rose,
the rose submerged,
the nocturnal,
the unsubstantial rose,
the void rose.
It is the rose of touch in darkness,
it is the rose that comes forward inflamed,
the rose of rosy nails,
the bud rose of eager fingertips,
the digital rose,
the blind rose.

It is the molded rose of hearing,
the ear rose,

la espiral del ruido,
la rosa concha siempre abandonada
en la más alta espuma de la almohada.

Es la rosa encarnada de la boca,
la rosa que habla despierta
como si estuviera dormida.
Es la rosa entreabierta
de la que mana sombra,
la rosa entraña
que se pliega y expande
evocada, invocada, abocada,
es la rosa labial,
la rosa herida.

Es la rosa que abre los párpados,
la rosa vigilante, desvelada,
la rosa del insomnio desojada.

Es la rosa del humo,
la rosa de ceniza,
la negra rosa de carbón diamante
que silenciosa horada las tinieblas
y no ocupa lugar en el espacio.

the noise's spiral,
the shell rose always left behind
in the loudest surf of the pillow.

It is the fleshed rose of the mouth,
the rose that, waking, speaks
as though it were sleeping.
It is the half-open rose
from out of which pours shade,
the entrail rose
that folds up and expands,
required, desired, devoured,
it is the labial rose,
the wounded rose.

It is the rose that opens its lids,
the vigilant, wakeful rose,
the shattered rose of insomnia.

It is the rose of smoke,
the ash rose,
the diamond coal's black rose
which, noiseless, drills through darkness
and occupies no point in space.

Translated by Donald Justice

Cementerio en la nieve

A nada puede compararse un cementerio en la nieve.
¿Qué nombre dar a la blancura sobre lo blanco?
El cielo ha dejado caer insensibles piedras de nieve
sobre las tumbas,
y ya no queda sino la nieve sobre la nieve
como la mano sobre sí misma eternamente posada.

Los pájaros prefieren atravesar el cielo,
herir los invisibles corredores del aire
para dejar sola la nieve,
que es como dejarla intacta,
que es como dejarla nieve.

Porque no basta decir que un cementerio en la nieve
es como un sueño sin sueños
ni como unos ojos en blanco.

Si algo tiene de un cuerpo insensible y dormido,
de la caída de un silencio sobre otro
y de la blanca persistencia del olvido,
¡a nada puede compararse un cementerio en la nieve!

Porque la nieve es sobre todo silenciosa,
más silenciosa aún sobre las losas exangües:
labios que ya no pueden decir una palabra.

Cemetery in the Snow

Nothing is like a cemetery in the snow.
What name is there for the whiteness upon the white?
The sky has let down insensible stones of snow
upon the tombs,
and all that is left now is snow upon snow
like a hand settled on itself forever.

Birds prefer to cut through the sky,
to wound the invisible corridors of the air
so as to leave the snow alone,
which is to leave it intact,
which is to leave it snow.

Because it is not enough to say that a cemetery in the snow
is like a sleep without dreams
or like a few blank eyes.

Though it is something like an insensible and sleeping body,
like one silence fallen upon another
and like the white persistence of oblivion,
nothing is like a cemetery in the snow!

Because the snow is above all silent,
more silent still upon bloodless slabs:
lips that can no longer say a word.

Translated by Donald Justice

JOSÉ GOROSTIZA
(nacido en Villahermosa, Tabasco 1901)

Ha sido embajador, delegado a conferencias internacionales, subsecretario y secretario de Asuntos Exteriores. Actualmente preside sobre la Comisión de Energía Nuclear. Ha publicado algunos volúmenes de poesía, siendo el más famoso *Muerte sin fin*.

Muerte sin fin
[*Fragmentos*]

Lleno de mí, sitiado en mi epidermis
por un dios inasible que me ahoga,
mentido acaso
por su radiante atmósfera de luces
que oculta mi conciencia derramada,
mis alas rotas en esquirlas de aire,
mi torpe andar a tientas por el lodo;
lleno de mí—ahito—me descubro
en la imagen atónita del agua,
que tan sólo es un tumbo inmarcesible,
un desplome de ángeles caídos
a la delicia intacta de su peso,
que nada tiene
sino la cara en blanco
hundida a medias, ya, como una risa agónica,
en las tenues holandas de la nube
y en los funestos cánticos del mar
—más resabio de sal o albor de cúmulo
que sola prisa de acosada espuma.
No obstante—oh paradoja—constreñida
por el rigor del vaso que la aclara,
el agua toma forma.
En él se asienta, ahonda y edifica,
cumple una edad amarga de silencios
y un reposo gentil de muerte niña,
sonriente, que desflora
un más allá de pájaros
en desbandada.
En la red de cristal que la estrangula,

JOSÉ GOROSTIZA
(born in Villahermosa, Tabasco, 1901)

Has been ambassador, delegate to international conferences, under-secretary and secretary of foreign affairs. Currently, he presides over the National Commission of Nuclear Energy. He has published several volumes of poetry, the most famous of which is *Muerte Sin Fin*.

FROM
Death Without End

Filled with myself, walled up in my skin
by an inapprehensible god that is stifling me,
deceived perhaps
by his radiant atmosphere of light
that hides my drained conscience,
my wings broken into splinters of air,
my listless groping through the mire;
filled with myself—gorged—I discover my essence
in the astonished image of water,
that is only an unwithering cascade,
a tumbling of angels fallen
of their own accord in pure delight,
that has nothing
but a whitened face
half sunken, already, like an agonized laugh
in the thin sheets of the cloud
and the mournful canticles of the sea—
more aftertaste of salt or cumulus whiteness
than lonely haste of foam pursued.
Nevertheless—oh paradox—constrained
by the rigor of the glass that clarifies it,
the water takes shape.
In the glass it sits, sinks deep and builds,
attains a bitter age of silences
and the graceful repose of a child smiling
in death, that deflowers
a beyond of disbanded
birds.
In the crystal snare that strangles it,

allí, como en el agua de un espejo,
se reconoce;
atada allí, gota a gota,
marchito el tropo de espuma en la garganta,
¡qué desnudez de agua tan intensa,
qué agua tan agua,
está en su orbe tornasol soñando,
cantando ya una sed de hielo justo!
¡Mas qué vaso—también—más providente
éste que así se hinche
como una estrella en grano,
que así, en heroica promisión, se enciende
como un seno habitado por la dicha,
y rinde así, puntual,
una rotunda flor
de transparencia al agua,
un ojo proyectil que cobra alturas
y una ventana a gritos luminosos
sobre esa libertad enardecida
que se agobia de cándidas prisiones!

there, as in the water of a mirror,
it recognizes itself;
bound there, drop with drop,
the trope of foam withered in its throat.
What intense nakedness of water,
what water so strongly water,
is dreaming in its iridescent sphere,
already singing a thirst for rigid ice!
But what a provident glass—also—
that swells
like a star ripe with grain,
that flames in heroic promise
like a heart inhabited by happiness,
and that punctually yields up
to the water
a round transparent flower,
a missile eye that attains heights
and a window to luminous cries
over that smoldering liberty
oppressed by white fetters!

Translated by Rachel Benson

MANUEL MAPLES ARCE
(*nacido Papantla, Veracruz 1900*)

Un diplomático de carrera, ha vivido en Europa, Asia, y América del
Sur. Ha escrito cuatro libros de poesía.

Urbe
[*Fragmento*]

Entre los matorrales del silencio
la oscuridad lame la sangre del crepúsculo.
Las estrellas caídas
son pájaros muertos
en el agua sin sueño
del espejo.

Y las artillerías
sonoras del atlántico
se apagaron,
al fin,
en la distancia.

        Sobre la arboladura del otoño,
        sopla un viento nocturno:
        es el viento de Rusia,
        de las grandes tragedias,

y el jardín,
amarillo,
se va a pique en la sombra.
Súbito, su recuerdo
chisporrotea en los interiores apagados.

        Sus palabras de oro
        criban en mi memoria.

Los ríos de blusas azules
desbordan las esclusas de las fábricas
y los árboles agitadores
manotean sus discursos en la acera.

MANUEL MAPLES ARCE

(born Papantla, Veracruz, 1900)

A career diplomat, he has lived in Europe, Asia and South America. He has written four books of poems.

City

In the thickets of silence
darkness laps up the blood of twilight.
Fallen stars
are dead birds
in the mirror's
sleepless water.

And the Atlantic's
loud artillery
was silenced
at last,
in the distance.

> Over the masts and spars of autumn,
> blows a nocturnal wind:
> it is the wind of Russia,
> of the great tragedies,

and the yellow
garden
founders in the dark.
Its memory suddenly
sparkles in the dimmed interiors.

> Its gold words
> pass through my mind.

Rivers of blue blouses
overflow the floodgates of factories
and the mutinous trees on the sidewalks
speak out in gestures.

Los huelguistas se arrojan
pedradas y denuestos,
y la vida es una tumultuosa
conversión hacia la izquierda.

Al margen de la almohada,
la noche es un despeñadero;
y el insomnio
se ha quedado escarbando en mi cerebro

¿De quién son esas voces
que sobrenadan en la sombra?

Y estos trenes que aúllan
hacia los horizontes devastados.

Los soldados
dormirán esta noche en el infierno.

Dios mío,
y de todo este desastre
sólo unos cuantos pedazos
blancos,
de su recuerdo,
se me han quedado entre las manos.

The strikers try
stone-throwing and insults
and life is a wild
conversion to the left.

At the pillow's edge,
night is a precipice
and insomnia
has kept picking at my brain.

Whose voices are these
that float in the darkness?

      And those trains that howl
      toward ruined horizons.

      The soldiers
      tonight will sleep in hell.

My God,
and from all this disaster
only some blank
bits
of its memory
have stayed in my hands.

Translated by Mark Strand

CARLOS PELLICER

(*nacido en Villahermosa, Tabasco 1899*)

Ganó el Premio Nacional de Literatura en 1964. El año siguiente fue elegido presidente de La Comunidad de Escritores de América Latina. Ha escrito muchos libros de poesía, todas aparecen en el volumen titulado *Material poético 1918–1961* publicado en 1962.

Estudio

a Pedro Henríquez Ureña

Jugaré con las casas de Curazao,
pondré el mar a la izquierda
y haré más puentes movedizos.
¡Lo que diga el poeta!
Estamos en Holanda y en América
y es una isla de juguetería,
con decretos de reina
y ventanas y puertas de alegría.
Con las cuerdas de la lira
y los pañuelos del viaje,
haremos velas para los botes
que no van a ninguna parte.
La casa de gobierno es demasiado pequeña
para una familia holandesa.
Por la tarde vendrá Claude Monet
a comer cosas azules y eléctricas.
Y por esa callejuela sospechosa
haremos pasar la *Ronda* de Rembrandt.
. . . pásame el puerto de Curazao!
      isla de juguetería,
      con decretos de reina
      y ventanas y puertas de alegría.

CARLOS PELLICER

(born in Villahermosa, Tabasco, 1899)

Winner of the Premio Nacional de Literatura in 1964, he was, in the following year, elected President of The Latin American Community of Writers. His many books of poems have been collected in a single volume, *Material Poético 1918–1961*, published in 1962.

Study

> *to Pedro Henríquez Ureña*

I shall play with the houses of Curaçao,
I shall put the sea on the left
and make more bridges that sway.
So says the poet!
We are in Holland and America too,
and this is a toyshop isle,
where the laws are a queen's
and doors and windows smile.
With the strings of the lyre
and the handkerchiefs of the voyage,
we shall make sails for boats
that never go anywhere.
Government House is far too small
for a Dutch family.
This evening Claude Monet will arrive
to eat blue and electric things.
And up this suspicious alley
we shall send Rembrandt's *Night Watch*.
. . . give me the port of Curaçao!
    toyshop isle,
    where the laws are a queen's
    and doors and windows smile.

Translated by Donald Justice

Recuerdos de Iza
(*Un pueblecito de los Andes*)

1. Creeríase que la población,
   después de recorrer el valle,
   perdió la razón
   y se trazó una sola calle.

2. Y así bajo la cordillera
   se apostó febrilmente como la primavera.

3. En sus ventanas el alcohol
   está mezclado con sol.

4. Sus mujeres y sus flores
   hablan el dialecto de los colores.

5. Y el riachuelo que corre como un caballo,
   arrastra las gallinas en febrero y en mayo.

6. Pasan por la acera
   lo mismo el cura, que la vaca y que la luz postrera.

7. Aquí no suceden cosas
   de mayor trascendencia que las rosas.

8. Como amenaza lluvia,
   se ha vuelto morena la tarde que era rubia.

9. Parece que la brisa
   estrena un perfume y un nuevo giro.

10. Un cantar me despliega una sonrisa
    y me hunde un suspiro.

Memories of Iza
(*A Small Town of the Andes*)

1. One might have thought the town,
   with the valley behind,
   had lost its mind
   and laid the one street down.

2. Likewise the mountains, row on row,
   feverishly, like the spring, got posted below.

3. The alcohol upon
   its windows is blended with sun.

4. Its women and its flowers
   speak the dialect of colors.

5. And the little stream that gallops away
   runs off with the hens February and May.

6. Up the sidewalk they go past,
   curate like cow, and the light going last.

7. Here nothing discloses
   a greater transcendence than the roses.

8. As rain begins to seem a threat,
   the once blond afternoon has gone brunette.

9. It seems the wind's
   using a new perfume as it turns around.

10. With a song my smile unbends
    and all my sighs are drowned.

Translated by Donald Justice

Deseos

a Salvador Novo

Trópico, para qué me diste
las manos llenas de color.
Todo lo que yo toque
se llenará de sol.
En las tardes sutiles de otras tierras
pasaré con mis ruidos de vidrio tornasol.
Déjame un solo instante
dejar de ser grito y color.
Déjame un solo instante
cambiar de clima el corazón,
beber la penumbra de una cosa desierta,
inclinarme en silencio sobre un remoto balcón,
ahondarme en el manto de pliegues finos,
dispersarme en la orilla de una suave devoción,
acariciar dulcemente las cabelleras lacias
y escribir con un lápiz muy fino mi meditación.
¡Oh, dejar de ser un solo instante
el Ayudante de Campo del sol!
¡Trópico, para qué me diste
las manos llenas de color!

Estudios

I
Relojes descompuestos,
   voluntarios caminos
sobre la música del tiempo.
   Hora y veinte.
Gracias a vuestro
paso
lento,
llego a las citas mucho después
y así me doy todo a las máquinas
gigantescas y translúcidas del silencio.

Wishes

to Salvador Novo

Tropics, why did you give me
these hands brimming with color?
Whatever I touch
brims over with sunlight.
I'll pass through the delicate afternoons of other lands
with the sound of a glass sunflower.
Let me for one moment
stop being all noise and color.
Let me for one moment
change the climate of my heart,
soak up the half-light of some solitary thing,
lean out from a distant balcony in silence,
sink deep into the fine folds of my cloak,
be strewn upon the bank of a quiet passion,
softly caress the long straight hair of women
and write my reflections out with a fine pencil.
Oh, for one moment not to be
Field Adjutant to the sun!
Tropics, why did you give me
these hands brimming with color!

Translated by Donald Justice

Studies

I
Clocks out of order,
    willful paths
across the music of time.
    Twenty past.
Thanks to your
slow
pace,
I arrive for appointments much later
and thus am completely given over
to the gigantic and translucent machines of silence.

II

Diez kilómetros sobre la vía
de un tren retrasado.
El paisaje crece
dividido de telegramas.
Las noticias van a tener tiempo
de cambiar de camisa.
La juventud se prolonga diez minutos,
el ojo caza tres sonrisas.
Kilo de panoramas
pagado con el tiempo
que se gana perdiendo.

III

Las horas se adelgazan;
de una salen diez.
Es el trópico,
prodigioso y funesto.
Nadie sabe qué hora es.

Poema Pródigo

a Luis Cardoza y Aragón

Gracias, ¡oh trópico!,
porque a la orilla caudalosa
y al ojo constelado
me traes de nuevo el pie del viaje.
(¡Esquinas de países que anuncian el paisaje!)
En mi casa de las nubes
o bajo el cielo de los árboles,
rodeado de todas las cosas creadas
(oídas espirales del berbiquí mirada),
voy y vengo sin tocar objeto alguno
—poseedor de la puerta y de la llave—
y de la alegre rama del trino.

II

Ten kilometers down the track
on a train behind schedule.
The landscape gets bigger,
divided by telegrams.
The news is going to have time
to change shirts.
Youth is prolonged ten minutes,
the eye catches three smiles.
A kilo of panoramas
paid for with the time
gained in being lost.

III

The hours grow thin;
out of one come ten.
These are the tropics,
prodigious and sad.
Nobody knows what time it is.

Translated by Donald Justice

Prodigal Poem

to Luis Cardoza y Aragón

Thank you, o tropics,
because to flowing shore
and sparkling spring
you lead my traveling foot once more.
(Corners of lands that announce the landscape!)
In my house of clouds
or under the sky roofed in by trees,
surrounded by all created things
(rumorous spiralings of the gimlet eye)
I come and go touching no object
—keeper of gate and key—
and the glad branch of song.

En la rápida pausa del antílope
se oyen las pausas lentas de la noche,
y en el desnudo torso y en los brazos que reman
tus fuerzas me saludan
brotantes
hacia otra parte siempre nueva.
Gracias,
porque en mis labios de treinta años
has puesto el gusto y el silencio
del fruto y de la flor.
Los grupos de palmeras
me sombrean la sed junto al desierto.
Y el invitado oasis
que brinda el vino siempre de los límites
tiene los labios gruesos de llamarme
y actos de bailarinas en reposo.
Voy en barca
entre arrecifes de granito.
Anclo y salto a una nube de alabastro.
El árbol de la goma
suscita el desbordar.
La hora oblicua se bisela a fondo.
Y yo surjo en el codo del camino
y canto en mí el principio de mi canto
y llego hasta mis labios
y soy mío.
Jocunda fe del trópico,
ojo dodecaedro,
¡justísimo sudor de no hacer nada!
Y el sabor de la vida de los siglos
y la orilla gentil y el pie del baño
y el poema.

In the brief pause of the antelope
are heard the long pauses of the night,
and with naked torso and a rower's arms
your forces salute me
shooting forth
always in new directions.
Thank you,
because on my lips and their thirty years
you have laid the flavor and the silence
of fruit and flower.
Palm groves
give shade to my thirst beside the desert.
And the welcome oasis
which proffers always the wine of its borders
has lips swollen with calling me
and scenes of dancing girls in repose.
I go by boat
between granite reefs.
I anchor and leap onto an alabaster cloud.
The rubber tree
quickens to overflowing.
The slanting hour is beveled perfectly.
And I come forth in the crook of the path
and I sing in myself the beginning of my song
and I get as far as my lips
and I am mine.
Bright faith of the tropics,
dodecahedron spring—
Oh, this most righteous sweat of doing nothing!
And salt of the life of the ages
and bountiful shore and bathing foot
and poem.

Translated by Donald Justice

JULIO TORRI
(*nacido en Saltillo, 1889*)

Por muchos años él ha sido profesor de literatura española a la Universidad Nacional Autónoma de Méjico. Ha escrito varios libros de poesía, siendo el mas reciente una selección de sus obras titulada *Tres Libros* (1964).

A Circe

¡Circe, diosa venerable! He seguido puntualmente tus avisos. Mas no me hice amarrar al mástil cuando divisamos la isla de las sirenas, porque iba resuelto a perderme. En medio del mar silencioso estaba la pradera fatal. Parecía un cargamento de violetas errante por las aguas.

¡Circe, noble diosa de los hermosos cabellos! Mi destino es cruel. Como iba resuelto a perderme, las sirenas no cantaron para mí.

JULIO TORRI
(*born in Saltillo, 1889*)

For many years a professor of Spanish Literature at the University of Mexico. He has written several books of poems, the most recent being a selection of his work entitled *Tres Libros* (1964).

Circe

Circe, venerable goddess! I have faithfully followed your advice. Do not tie me to the mast when we approach the island of the sirens, it would be my ruin. In the middle of the silent ocean I saw the fatal fields. They seemed like a cargo of violets wandering on the waters.

Circe of flowing hair, noble goddess! My destiny is cruel. How was it going to be my ruin, the sirens did not sing to me.

Translated by Mark Strand

Mujeres

Siempre me descubro reverente al paso de las mujeres elefantas, maternales, castísimas, perfectas.

Sé del sortilegio de las mujeres reptiles—los labios fríos, los ojos zarcos—que nos miran sin curiosidad ni comprensión desde otra especie zoológica.

Convulso, no recuerdo si de espanto o atracción, he conocido un raro ejemplar de mujeres tarántulas. Por misteriosa adivinación de su verdadera naturaleza vestía siempre de terciopelo negro. Tenía las pestañas largas y pesadas, y sus ojillos de bestezuela cándida me miraban con simpatía casi humana.

Las mujeres asnas son la perdición de los hombres superiores. Y los cenobitas secretamente piden que el diablo no revista tan terrible apariencia en la hora mortecina de las tentaciones.

Y tú, a quien las acompasadas dichas del matrimonio han metamorfoseado en lucia vaca que rumia deberes y faenas, y que miras con tus grandes ojos el amanerado paisaje donde paces, cesa de mugir amenazadora al incauto que se acerca a tu vida, no como el tábano de la fábula antigua, sino llevado por veleidades de naturalista curioso.

Women

I always discover myself reverent at the passing of elephantine women, maternal, female, perfect.

I know the sorcery of reptilian women—the cold lips, the crystal eyes—that look at us without curiosity or comprehension from another zoological specie.

Conversely, I don't recall whether with fright or attraction, I have known a rare example of female tarantula. By mysterious divination of their true natures they dressed always in black velvet. They had long and heavy eyelashes and their big eyes of the sort little beasts possess looked at me with almost human sympathy.

Female donkeys are the downfall of the superior male. And monks secretly ask that the devil not bring up the terrible apparition of temptation in the hour of death.

And you, whom the measured refrains of marriage have metamorphosed into a glowing cow that chews its cud and does its duty, and that looks at the perfect landscape where it grazes, cease to low threateningly at the careless who come too close to your life, not like the gadfly of old fables, but spurred on by the feebleness of natural curiosity.

Translated by Mark Strand

RAMÓN LÓPEZ VELARDE
(*nacido en Jerez, Zacatecas 1888, fallecido en Méjico 1921*)

Estudió en Zacatecas y Aguascalientes, fué recibido de abogado en
San Luis Potosí, pasó mucho de su tiempo como profesor de literatura.
Publicó muchos libros de poesía y *Poesías completas,* una recolección
de sus poemas, fué publicado en 1953.

Mi prima Águeda

   a Jesús Villalpando

Mi madrina invitaba a mi prima Águeda
a que pasara el día con nosotros,
y mi prima llegaba
con un contradictorio
prestigio de almidón y de temible
luto ceremonioso.

Águeda aparecía, resonante
de almidón, y sus ojos
verdes y sus mejillas rubicundas
me protegían contra el pavoroso
luto . . .
        Yo era rapaz
y conocía la *o* por lo redondo,
y Águeda, que tejía
mansa y perseverante en el sonoro
corredor, me causaba
calosfríos ignotos . . .
(Creo que hasta la debo la costumbre
heroicamente insana de hablar solo.)
A la hora de comer, en la penumbra
quieta del refectorio,
me iba embelesando un quebradizo
sonar intermitente de vajilla
y el timbre caricioso
de la voz de mi prima.
        Águeda era
(luto, pupilas verdes y mejillas

RAMÓN LÓPEZ VELARDE

(born Jerez, Zacatecas, 1888, died Mexico, D.F., 1921)

Studied in Zacatecas and Aguascalientes, was admitted to the bar in
San Luis Potosí, spent much of his time as a professor of literature. He
published many books of poetry and *Poesias Completas*, his collected
poems, was published in 1953.

My Cousin Agatha

to Jesús Villalpando

My godmother used to invite my cousin Agatha
to spend the day with us
and my cousin would arrive
dressed in a contradiction
of starch and terrible
ceremonious black.

Agatha would appear, rustling
with starch, and her green
eyes and ruddy cheeks
protected me against the awful
black . . .
           I was young
and knew the *o* by its roundness,
and Agatha knitting
meekly and perseveringly in the echoing
corridor gave me
unknown chills . . .
(I'm sure that to this day I owe to her
my heroically insane habit of talking alone.)
At dinnertime, in the quiet
half-light of the dining room,
I was captivated by a brittle
intermittent ringing of dishes
and the endearing timbre
of my cousin's voice.
              Agatha was
(black, green pupils and ruddy

rubicundas) un cesto policromo
de manzanas y uvas
en el ébano de un armario añoso.

Hormigas

A la cálida vida que transcurre canora
con garbo de mujer sin letras ni antifaces,
a la invicta belleza que salva y que enamora,
responde, en la embriaguez de la encantada hora,
un encono de hormigas en mis venas voraces.

Fustigan el desmán del perenne hormigueo
el pozo del silencio y el enjambre del ruido,
la harina rebanada como doble trofeo
en los fértiles bustos, el Infierno en que creo,
el estertor final y el preludio del nido.

Mas luego mis hormigas me negarán su abrazo
y han de huir de mis pobres y trabajados dedos
cual se olvida en la arena un gélido bagazo;
y tu boca, que es cifra de eróticos denuedos,
tu boca, que es mi rúbrica, mi manjar y mi adorno,
tu boca, en que la lengua vibra asomada al mundo
como réproba llama saliéndose de un horno,
en una turbia fecha de cierzo gemebundo
en que ronde la luna porque robarte quiera,
ha de oler a sudario y a hierba machacada,
a droga y a responso, a pábilo y a cera.

Antes de que deserten mis hormigas, Amada,
dájalas caminar camino de tu boca
a que apuren los viáticos del sanguinario fruto
que desde sarracenos oasis me provoca.

Antes de que tus labios mueran, para mi luto,
dámelos en el crítico umbral del cementerio
como perfume y pan y tósigo y cauterio.

cheeks) a polychrome basket
of apples and grapes
on the ebony of an aged cabinet.

Translated by Douglas Eichhorn

Ants

To the warm life gliding musically by
with the grace of a woman with no schooling nor veils,
to the unconquered beauty that saves and enamors,
in the intoxication of an enchanted hour,
a rash of ants in my ravenous veins responds.

The well of silence and the swarm of noise,
the flour split like a double trophy
into fertile busts, the Hell I believe in,
the last death rattle and the prelude to the nest—
all lash the excess of my incessant itching.

But soon my ants will deny me their embrace
and will have to flee my poor and overworked fingers
like the gelid residue of sugar cane left on sand;
and your mouth, which is a cipher of erotic ventures,
your mouth, which is my rubric, my morsel, my adornment,
your mouth, with its quivering tongue sticking out at the world
like a reprobate flame escaping from a furnace,
on a murky day with the north wind groaning
and the moon out prowling because it wants to steal you away,
will smell of winding sheet and trampled grass,
of drug and graveside prayer, of wick and candlewax.

Before my ants desert, Love,
let them wind their way along your mouth
that they may drain the viaticums from the bloodthirsty fruit
that summons me from a Saracen oasis.

Before your lips die, for me to grieve over,
give them to me at the critical threshold of the cemetery,
like perfume and bread and poison and cautery.

Translated by Douglas Eichhorn

El candil

a Alejandro Quijano

En la cúspide radiante
que el metal de mi persona
dilucida y perfecciona,
y en que una mano celeste
y otra de tierra me fincan
sobre la sien la corona;
en la orgía matinal
en que me ahogo en azul
y soy como un esmeril
y central y esencial como el rosal;
en la gloria en que melifluo
soy activamente casto
porque lo vivo y lo inánime
se me ofrece gozoso como pasto;
en esta mística gula
en que mi nombre de pila
es una candente cábala
que todo lo engrandece y lo aniquila;
he descubierto mi símbolo
en el candil en forma de bajel
que cuelga de las cúpulas criollas
su cristal sabio y su plegaria fiel.

¡Oh candil, oh bajel, frente al altar
cumplimos, en dúo recóndito,
un solo mandamiento: venerar!

Embarcación que iluminas
a las piscinas divinas:
en tu irisada presencia
mi humanidad se esponja y se anaranja,
porque en la muda eminencia
están anclados contigo
el vuelo de mis gaviotas
y el humo sollozante de mis flotas.

¡Oh candil, oh bajel: Dios ve tu pulso
y sabe que te anonadas

The Chandelier

to Alejandro Quijano

In the radiant spire
that my personal essence
illuminates and perfects,
and where a hand from heaven
and another from earth
set the crown upon my temple;
in the orgy of morning
where drowning in blue
I am like emery
and central and essential as the rosebush;
in the glory where, mellifluous,
I am diligently chaste
because the alive and the lifeless
are joyfully offered me as nourishment;
in this mystic gluttony
where my Christian name
is an incandescent cabal
enlarging and annihilating all;
I have discovered my symbol
in the chandelier formed like a ship
dangling its shrewd crystal and earnest prayer
from creole domes.

O chandelier, o ship, before the altar
we, a secret pair, fulfill
a single commandment: worship!

Vessel, you who give light
to divine basins:
in your clear presence
my humanity swells and oranges,
for in mute eminence
the flight of my gulls
and the sobbing smoke from my fleets
are anchored to you.

O chandelier, o ship: God sees your pulsing
and knows you are humbled—

en las cúpulas sagradas
no por decrépito ni por insulso!
Tu alta oración animas
con el genio de los climas.

Tú no conoces el espanto
de las islas de leprosos,
el domicilio polar
de los donjuanescos osos,
la magnética bahía
de los deliquios venéreos,
las garzas ecuatoriales
cual escrúpulos aéreos,
y por ello ante el Señor
paralizas tu experiencia
como el olor que da tu mejor flor.

Paralelo a tu quimera,
cristalizo sin sofismas
las brasas de mi ígnea primavera,
enarbolo mi júbilo y mi mal
y suspendo mis llagas como prismas.

Candil, que vas como yo
enfermo de lo absoluto,
y enfilas la experta proa
a un dorado archipiélago sin luto;
candil, hermético esquife:
mis sueños recalcitrantes
enmudecen cual un cero
en tu cristal marinero,
inmóviles, excelsos y adorantes.

not for being old nor tarnished—
in the sacred domes!

You brighten your high prayer
with the spirit of these regions.

You do not know the terror
of islands of lepers,
the polar home
of Don Juanish bears,
the magnetic bay
of sexual swoons,
the equatorial cranes
like scruples in flight,
and so before the Lord
you paralyze what you know
like the odor given off by your best flower.

Like your chimera,
I crystallize without deception
the hot coals of my igneous spring,
hoist my joy and sickness on high
and hang my wounds like prisms.

Chandelier, you who like me
are sick of the absolute,
and point your expert prow
toward a golden archipelago without grief;
chandelier, magical skiff:
my recalcitrant dreams
grow hushed as a zero
on your seaworthy crystal,
still, lofty and reverent.   *Translated by Douglas Eichhorn*

Humildemente . . .

a mi madre y a mis hermanas

Cuando me sobrevenga
el cansancio del fin,
me iré, como la grulla
del refrán, a mi pueblo,
a arrodillarme entre
las rosas de la Plaza,
los aros de los niños
y los flecos de seda de los tápalos.

A arrodillarme en medio
de una banqueta herbosa,
cuando sacramentando
al reloj de la torre,
de redondel de luto
y manecillas de oro,
al hombre y a la bestia,
al azahar que embriaga
y a los rayos del sol,
aparece en su estufa el Divinísimo.

Abrazado a la luz
de la tarde que borda,
como al hilo de una
apostólica araña,
he de decir mi prez
humillada y humilde,
más que las herraduras
de las mansas acémilas
que conducen al Santo Sacramento.
"Te conozco, Señor,
aunque viajas de incógnito,
y a tu paso de aromas
me quedo sordomudo,
paralítico y ciego,
por gozar tu balsámica presencia.

Humbly

to my mother and my sisters

When the last weariness
comes over me,
I shall go to my village,
like the crane in the story,
to kneel among
the roses in the plaza,
the hoops of the children
and the silk fringes of the shawls.

To kneel in the midst
of a grassy banquet
when, hallowing all—
the belfry clock
with face in morning
and gold hands,
and man and beast,
and the dizzying blossom
of orange and of lemon,
and the rays of the sun—
appears in his carriage the Most High.

Entwined in the light
the afternoon weaves,
as in some apostolical
spider's thread,
I must speak of my worth,
humbled and humble,
more so than the shoes
of the docile mules
on the way to the Blessed Sacrament.

"I know you, Lord,
though you go in disguise,
and your scented tread
leaves me deaf and dumb,
palsied and blind,
for joy of your balsamic presence.

"Tu carroza sonora
apaga repentina
el breve movimiento,
cual si fuesen las calles
una juguetería
que se quedó sin cuerda.

"Mi prima, con la aguja
en alto, tras sus vidrios,
está inmóvil con un gesto de estatua.

"El cartero aldeano
que trae nuevas del mundo
se ha hincado en su valija.

"El húmedo corpiño
de Genoveva, puesto
a secar, ya no baila
arriba del tejado.

"La gallina y sus pollos
pintados de granizo
interrumpen su fábula.

"La frente de don Blas
petrificóse junto
a la hinchada baldosa
que agrietan las raíces de los fresnos.

"Las naranjas cesaron
de crecer, y yo apenas
si palpito a tus ojos
para poder vivir este minuto.

"Señor, mi temerario
corazón que buscaba
arrogantes quimeras
se anonada y te grita
que yo soy tu juguete agradecido.'

"Your sounding chariot
stifles at once
the brief commotion,
as though the streets were
filled with puppets
without their strings.

"My cousin, her needle poised,
behind her window glass,
stands in a statuesque pose, transfixed.

"The village postman,
who brings news of the world,
has knelt on his mailbag.

"Genevieve's damp corset,
hung out to dry,
no longer dances
above the shed.

"The white-speckled hen
and her brood of chicks
cut short their fable.

"The brow of Don Blas
grew petrified next
to the buckled flagstone
split apart by the roots of the ash trees.

"The oranges stopped growing,
and I scarcely,
before your gaze,
throb with the power to live through this moment.

"Lord, my rash heart
that went in search of
proud chimeras,
abases itself
and cries that I am your grateful puppet.

"Porque me acompasaste
en el pecho un imán
de figura de trébol
y apasionada tinta de amapola.

"Pero ese mismo imán
es humilde y oculto,
como el peine imantado
con que las señoritas
levantan alfileres
y electrizan su pelo en la penumbra.

"Señor, este juguete
de corazón de imán,
te ama y te confiesa
con el íntimo ardor
de la raíz que empuja
y agrieta las baldosas seculares.

"Todo está de rodillas
y en el polvo las frentes;
mi vida es la amapola
pasional, y su tallo
doblégase efusivo
para morir debajo de tus ruedas."

El sueño de los guantes negros

Soñé que la ciudad estaba dentro
del más bien muerto de los mares muertos.
Era una madrugada del invierno
y lloviznaban gotas de silencio.

No más señal viviente que los ecos
de una llamada a misa, en el misterio
de una capilla oceánica, a lo lejos.

De súbito me sales al encuentro,
resucitada y con tus guantes negros.

"Because in my breast
you fixed a magnet
with the shape of a clover
and the passionate color of a poppy.

"But that very magnet
is humble and hidden,
like the magnetized comb
with which young ladies
lift hairpins up
and electrify their hair in the lamplight.

"Lord, this puppet
with magnet heart
loves and confesses you
with the intimate warmth
of the root pushing up
and splitting apart the ancient flagstones.

"All are kneeling,
their brows in the dust;
and my life is
the passional poppy,
whose stem bends down,
effusive, to die beneath your wheels."

Translated by Donald Justice

The Dream of the Black Gloves

I dreamed the city lay within
the very deadest of dead seas.
It was an early winter morning
and drops of silence drizzled down.

No sign of life but for the echoes
of mass bells tolling for some rite
in an oceanic chapel, far away.

Suddenly you come out to meet me,
brought back to life and wearing your black gloves.

Para volar a ti, le dio su vuelo
el Espíritu Santo a mi esqueleto.

Al sujetarme con tus guantes negros
me atrajiste al océano de tu seno,
y nuestras cuatro manos se reunieron
en medio de tu pecho y de mi pecho,
como si fueran los cuatro cimientos
de la fábrica de los universos.

¿Conservabas tu carne en cada hueso?
El enigma de amor se veló entero
en la prudencia de tus guantes negros.

¡Oh, prisionera del valle de México!
Mi carne . . .* de tu ser perfecto
quedarán ya tus huesos en mis huesos;
y el traje, el traje aquel, con que tu cuerpo
fue sepultado en el valle de México;
y el figurín aquel, de pardo género
que compraste en un viaje de recreo . . .

Pero en la madrugada de mi sueño,
nuestras manos, en un circuito eterno,
la vida apocalíptica vivieron.

Un fuerte . . . como en un sueño,
libre como cometa, y en su vuelo
la ceniza y . . . del cementerio
gusté cual rosa . . .

* Los puntos suspensivos indican palabras ilegibles en el original.

That I might fly to you, the Holy Ghost
lent to my skeleton His wings.

Holding me fast with your black gloves,
you lured me to the ocean of your breast,
and our four hands were reunited
midway between your bosom and my own,
as if they were the four foundations
supporting the framework of the galaxies.

Your flesh, was it preserved upon each bone?
The dark question of love was guarded by
the total prudence of your black gloves.

Oh, prisoner of the Valley of Mexico!
My flesh . . .° of your perfection
will remain now bone of my bone;
and the dress, that dress, in which your body
was laid to rest in the Valley of Mexico;
and that mannequin, made of some dark stuff
you picked up on a pleasure trip . . .

But in the early morning of my dream,
our hands, on an eternal circuit,
lived the apocalyptic life.

A strong . . . as though in a dream,
free as a comet, and on its flight
the ashes and . . . of the cemetery
seemed pleasing to me as a rose . . .

Translated by Donald Justice

° Note: the ellipses indicate illegible passages in the original text.

JOSÉ JUAN TABLADA
(nacido en Méjico D.F. 1871, fallecido en Nueva York 1945)

El primer poeta "moderno" de Méjico, fue también amigo y campeón de Diego Rivera y José Clemente Orozco y fue responsable de una sección de la cantata de Edgar Varèse, "Offrandes". El introdujo tanto el "hiku" como el "ideograph" en Méjico.

El pavo real

Pavo real, largo fulgor,
por el gallinero demócrata
pasas como una procesión . . .

Los sapos

Trozos de barro,
por la senda en penumbra
saltan los sapos.

Hojas secas

El jardín está lleno de hojas secas;
nunca vi tantas hojas en sus árboles
verdes, en primavera.

JOSÉ JUAN TABLADA
(born Mexico, D.F., 1871, died New York, 1945)

Mexico's first "modern" poet, he was also a friend and defender of
Diego Rivera and José Clemente Orozco, and responsible for a sec-
tion of Edgar Varese's cantata *Offrandes*. He introduced both the
haiku and the ideograph to Mexico.

The Peacock

Peacock, drawn out shimmer,
you pass like a procession
through the democratic henyard . . .

Translated by Hardie St. Martin

The Toads

Chunks of mud,
the toads hop
down the unlighted path.

Translated by Hardie St. Martin

Dry Leaves

The garden is full of dry leaves.
I never saw that many leaves
on the trees, when they were green, in the spring.

Translated by W. S. Merwin

Mariposa nocturna

Devuelve a la desnuda rama,
nocturna mariposa,
las hojas secas de tus alas.

El mono

El pequeño mono me mira . . .
¡Quisiera decirme
algo que se le olvida!

Panorama

Bajo de mi ventana, la luna en los tejados
y las sombras chinescas
y la música china de los gatos.

Peces voladores

Al golpe del oro solar
estalla en astillas el vidrio del mar.

NIGHT MOTH

Night moth,
return the dry leaves of your wings
to the stripped branch.

Translated by Hardie St. Martin

The Monkey

The little monkey throws me a look . . .
He wants to tell me something
he can't think of now!

Translated by Hardie St. Martin

Panorama

Under my window the moon on the roofs
and the Chinese shadows
and the cats' Chinese music.

Translated by W. S. Merwin

Flying Fish

Struck by the sun's gold
the pane of the sea bursts into splinters.

Translated by W. S. Merwin

Nocturno alterno

Neoyorquina noche dorada
    Fríos muros de cal moruna
Rector's champaña fox-trot
    Casas mudas y fuertes rejas
Y volviendo la mirada
    Sobre las silenciosas tejas
El alma petrificada
    Los gatos blancos de la luna
Como la mujer de Loth

    Y sin embargo
      es una
        misma
          en New York
            y en Bogotá

        la Luna . . . !

La Cruz del Sur

Las mujeres de gestos de madrépora
tienen pelos y labios rojo-orquídea.
Los monos del Polo son albinos
ámbar y nieve y saltan
vestidos de aurora boreal

En el cielo hay un anuncio
de Óleo-margarina
He aquí el Árbol de la quinina
y la Virgen de los Dolores
el Zodiaco gira en la noche
de fiebre amarilla
la lluvia encierra todo el trópico
en una jaula de cristal

Alternating Nocturne

New York night gold
    Cold walls of Moorish lime
Rector's foxtrot champagne
    Mute houses and strong gates
And gazing back
    Over the silent roofs
The petrified soul
    The white cats of the moon
Like the wife of Lot

    And nevertheless
      it is always
        the same
          in New York
            or Bogotá

        Moon . . . !

Translated by Eliot Weinberger

Southern Cross

Those women with sea-coral movements
have orchid-red hair and lips.
The monkeys at the Pole are albino
amber and snow they dance up and down
dressed in the aurora borealis

There's an Oleomargarine
ad in the sky
Here we have the quinine tree
and Our Lady of Sorrows
the Zodiac wheels around in the night
of yellow fever
rain keeps all the tropics
in a glass cage

Es la hora de atravesar el crepúsculo
como una cebra hacia la Isla de Antaño
donde despiertan las mujeres asesinadas

It's time to streak across the dusk
like a zebra toward the Island of Lastyear
where the murdered women break sleep

Translated by Hardie St. Martin

INDEX OF AUTHORS

182

INDEX OF FIRST LINES—SPANISH

He aquí que estamos reunidos 72

Jugaré con las casas de Curazao, 142

La creación está de pie, 52
La luz final que hará 50
la melena del león cubre el zoológico del cielo 46
La que acoge y conforta 58
Las cosas que entran por el silencio empiezan a llegar al cuarto. Lo 114
Las mujeres de gestos de madrépora 176
Lleno de mí, sitiado en mi epidermis 134

Mi amada es una tierra agradecida 48
Mi madrina invitaba a mi prima Águeda 156
Mientras los niños crecen, tú, con todos los muertos 74
Mientras tomo una taza de café repaso los poemas 36
Mis pasos en esta calle 102
Mueve los aires, torna en fuego 88

Nada más que horror, espacio puro y vacío. Eso es la caverna de Tribenciano 80
Neoyorquina noche dorada 176
no vino a despedirse 38

Pavo real, largo fulgor, 172

Rápidas manosffrías 102
Relojes des compuestos, 146

Salta de vez en cuando, sólo para comprobar su radical estático. El 84
Si alguien te dice que no es cierto, 68
Siempre me descubro reverente al paso de las mujeres elefantas, maternales 154
Soñar, soñar la noche, la calle, la escalera 124
Soñé que la ciudad estaba dentro 168

Tarumba. 64
Te puse una cabeza sobre el hombro 70
Todo el mundo está en llamas: lo visible 34
Trópico, para qué me diste 146
Trozos de barro, 172

Una tarde con árboles, 50

Vamos a cantar: 72

Verde o azul, fruto del muro, crece; 32

Y después, aquí, en el oscuro seno del río más oscuro, 90
Yo no lo sé de cierto, pero lo supongo 62
Yo también hablo de la rosa. 128

INDEX OF FIRST LINES—ENGLISH